Praise for *Live with* and Mary Anne R

"Mary Anne Radmacher has written a book of beau will. Her chapter on forgiveness alone is worth the p
— Hugh Prather, author of *Morning Notes* and *The Little Book of Letting Go*

"Many years ago, I bought a framed poster of 'Live with Intention,' the inspiring phrase by Mary Anne Radmacher. It has hung on my wall ever since, in seven different houses. I have since bought and read every book she has written. Mary Anne's newest book is beautiful, artistic, inspiring, and written from her heart."
— Dr. Patrick Williams, master certified coach and co-author of *Becoming a Professional Life Coach: Lessons from the Institute for Life Coach Training* and *Total Life Coaching: 50+ Life Lessons, Skills, and Techniques to Enhance Your Practice and Your Life*

"*Live with Intention* showed up at the perfect moment in my life, when I needed to be reminded to recommit to 'the promises I make to myself.' This book is filled with wisdom and can be read daily as a reminder that we create our lives each day, anew. Mary Anne graciously shares her philosophy and her life stories to show us the way to a life crafted by choices. This book is a treasure chest of ideas which will empower and enrich your future."
— Gail McMeekin, LICSW, author of *The 12 Secrets of Highly Creative Women* and *The Power of Positive Choices*

"Mary Anne Radmacher is the messenger of our hearts. And *Live with Intention* is the perfect message for this moment."
— Janet Conner, author of *Writing Down Your Soul: How to Activate and Listen to the Extraordinary Voice Within*

"Accessible, grounded, joyful, and wise, Mary Anne Radmacher's *Live with Intention* is pure gift, especially if you're looking for a practical yet visionary map of contemporary life. Pick up this gem and bask in insight after insight, all of which are solidly based on the realities of 21st-century life. And it always seems like you're simply chatting with your best friend. Great graphics, too."
— David Kundtz, author of *Awakened Mind: One-Minute Wake Up Calls*

Live with Intention

Live with Intention

rediscovering what we deeply know

mary anne radmacher

Conari Press

First published in 2011 by Conari Press
an imprint of Red Wheel/Weiser, LLC

With offices at:
500 Third Street, Suite 230
San Francisco, CA 94107
www.redwheelweiser.com

"Prayers Like Shoes" reprinted from *Prayers Like Shoes* (Whit Press, *www.whitpress.org*)
by Ruth Forman ©2009 Ruth Forman
Reprinted with permission of the author and the publisher

ISBN: 978-1-57324-401-5

Library of Congress Cataloging-in-Publlication Data is available on request.

Cover and interior design by Liz Kalloch
Typset in Adobe Garamond, Charlotte Sans and ITC Novarese
Cover. illustration, and hand lettering © Mary Anne Radmacher
Dedication image used with permission of Quotable Cards, Inc.
www.quotablecards.com

Cover photograph © Michael Stadler

Printed in Hong Kong
GWP
10 9 8 7 6 5 4 3 2 1

Dedication

Gillian and Matt

Thank you for letting my words hang out in such great company.
You took your love of words and brought mine to the world
with graphic beauty and immediacy. I am forever grateful to you
for broadcasting my words around the world
through the vehicle of Quotable Cards.

live with intention.
walk to the edge.
listen hard. practice
wellness. play with
abandon. laugh.
choose with no regret.
continue to learn.
appreciate your
friends. do what you
love. live as if this is
all there is.

~mary anne
radmacher

Contents

In which . . .

Introduction   1

. . . rediscovering what we deeply know is introduced and practical ways to remember are unfolded. "Be the center of your own flame."

Chapter 1: Completion - walk to the edge   15

. . . everything that overwhelms a day is put in the context of simple beginnings (or simply beginning). "Call them targeted completion dates."

Chapter 2: Spirit - listen hard   29

. . . many ways of listening, seeing, hearing are explored. "In the practiced pause, you can learn to listen."

Chapter 3: Health - practice wellness   41

. . . choices and opportunities are held to a different light and self nurturing is partnered with accountability for personal transformation. "Vitality has many different measures and weights."

Chapter 4: Play - play with abandon   53

. . . the apparent contradiction of play being both a serious matter and whimsically essential for just about everything that is inventive is considered. "Some days are simply meant for playing."

Chapter 5: Gratitude - laugh   63

. . . the many things that "have gone right" and the beneficial elements of living free of the past and obligation are celebrated. "We laugh to survive."

Chapter 6: **Forgiveness** - *choose with no regret*   71
. . . forgiving as a gift we give ourselves is explored and some
perspective shifts are suggested. "Embrace yourself as you are."

Chapter 7: **Enthusiasm** - *continue to learn*   85
. . . spirited vitality and willingness to learn are seen as partners and
pretending is presented as an essential skill set. "What if I just acted
as if everything was easy?"

Chapter 8: **Relationship** - *appreciate your friends*   95
. . . we observe that beautiful circles radiate outward from the core
relationship we maintain - the friendship we have to ourselves. "If
you have one friend, you hold the hand of the world."

Chapter 9: **Dream** - *do what you love*   109
. . . a journey to the place of awakening our dreams is taken and we
see the first step is doing what you love (and loving what you do).
"Dream like you know where you're going."

Chapter 10: **Generosity** - *live as if this is all there is*   125
. . . gifts and giving are extended in many forms and we travel to
where simply being utterly attentive to the moment is a generosity
of spirit. "Enlist in the company of angels."

afterword   141
. . . we peek into the gentle synchronicities of an ordinary day and
the words of a visiting poet are welcomed. "Much of our lives is
mystery."

acknowledgments   147

Introduction

If we do everything else but that one thing,
we will be lost. And if we do nothing else but that one thing,
we will have lived a glorious life.

—Rumi

live with intention.
walk to the edge.
listen hard.
practice wellness.
play with abandon.
laugh.
choose with no regret
continue to learn.
appreciate your friends
do what you love.
live as if this is
all there is.

This poem contains ten elements that summarize my "one thing." How I want to live my life. When I ask people to identify ten components that enliven them, that improve their day, that make their heart sing . . . consistently they identify things amazingly close to the elements in *Live with Intention*. I love that the word "intention" has the "ten" just built right in!

I take Rumi's reference to the "one thing" to mean the collection of elements, activities, attitudes, and actions that enliven and invigorate an intentional life.

The number ten is a model here for that reason. You might have eleven. Or nine. The most significant aspect is not that you specifically identify ten things, but that you identify and remember what your core elements are. Remember and actively live with your intentions. Invite those things into your experience consciously and daily. That's the way it really works. Those intentions—the collective one of them—are your "one thing." Maybe you want to investigate your own things. Go ahead. I have suggestions for you. But I know with certainty that if you pay attention to any one to ten of the things outlined here—your day will be the better for it. And, ultimately, your life will be better.

It is easy to grow into forgetting. Forgetting our personal priorities. Forgetting the things that bring us zip, verve, and fundamental joys. We roll into the habit of meeting the expectations of others, seeking approval by fitting in and, in general, responding to a status quo that is not resonant with our souls. How do we remember those things that have been set aside, disregarded, or positioned last on the "list"?

Live with Intention is a resource for you. I want to provoke and inspire you to rediscover that which you know deeply within yourself but allow the press of daily demands and uncertainties of life to kick out of your view. This is a safe place to be prompted in reflection and ruminations. It is a way to help you remember what you have temporarily overlooked or forgotten. Rediscovering, reconnecting to your intentions, whether they are similar to mine or completely different, will restore, renew, and bring to the forefront the life that you long to live. As you consider the diverse words gathered here, may you revel in the remembering (or discovering) of the intentional things that animate and invigorate your days.

How do you do that? Observe your life. Watch how your days unfold. Notice what invigorates or inspires you. Pay particular attention to the things for which you have unbounded energy and excitement. Making a list of these things is especially helpful. Some things are so deeply embedded into our experience, it can be difficult to see them. Part of this observation process involves being aware of what tires you, burns you out in an undesirable way. Perhaps there are events in which you are regularly involved that seem significant, but upon closer examination, you find actually drag you down, rather than elevate you. Many discover that their most significant intentions get the least amount of attention. Oddly, the "one thing" to which Rumi makes reference is often the last thing on lists of things to do. It is that proverbial carrot that is saved for a someday that hardly ever comes.

Do you know the one thing or the collection of things that together comprise the "one thing" that invigorates all your actions and sets you on fire? If you know it, do you measure the activities and focus of your day by it? If you do not know it, how do you make decisions and what do you measure them against?

Over a period of a week or a month, watch how you make decisions. To what do you dedicate your time and attention? Learn from those things to which you say yes and those that receive your "No, thank you." It is helpful to make notes on a daily basis. At the end of your observation period, you can draw certain conclusions. Categorize the events that both invigorate and drain you. Consider the balance between them and follow those threads to discover your intentions . . . *your one thing.*

In *Live with Intention*, you will find what I like to call my Word Birds—winged thoughts that fly out of my daily experience and come to roost as poetry—reflections on ordinary things that produce extraordinary shifts in the way the day shines, poems, promises I make to myself, observations, and remarkable words borrowed from others. In this collection of intentional things, I long for you to find the kernels of inspiration that will light up your ten things (or the things that comprise your "one thing") and help you remember or perhaps uncover what is held deeply inside you.

My friend Sandra seriously gave thought to her own intentions and what they might look like on an average day. Inspired by my list, she created her own "ten intentional things" list, as I hope you will. I'll share Sandra's with you:

1. Wake up rested, say my prayers, and give thanks for an opportunity to live another day.

2. Quiet time in the morning to wake up and start the morning with Peace and music.

3. Prepare and eat healthy food throughout the day.

4. Exercise.

5. Complete daily to-do lists and any additional chores.

6. Plan time for friends and family, do something fun.

7. Read a good book or magazines.

8. Learn something new, work, make a contribution to the world.

9. Write something every day.

10. Finish my day with prayers and gratitude.

This book is all the result of actively living out what I believe. It is practical. My life is not perfectly ordered, nor am I without challenges or difficulties. Yet I actively commit to these elements in each of my days. Some days contain more of them than others. Balance and ease of cadence do not always come easily to me, and that is why I have created systems to help bring clarity, verve, and balance to my life. I have created these systems for myself because, at the end of each day, that is what makes sense to me. And, at the end of nearly every day, I fall into a peaceful and deep sleep, content that I have invested that day with my finest intentions. Even those most challenging of days are made better when I willfully include these intentions in the course of my day. I am confident you will find that to be true for yourself as well. I lovingly share my experiences with you, knowing that you will consider my words and take what works for you and adjust it to fit the roads of your own life journey.

This book is written with love, earnest observation, and keen awareness that my life is richer for remembering my core intentions than it would be if I allowed the press of the world and the specific challenges of my life to overtake or overwhelm me. Staying connected to the core intentions of my life allows me to feel and be satisfied at the end of each day.

Set aside dogma and allow your doctrine to be defined by the way you embrace your day. Would you know what you believe? Watch yourself live. Hear the stories you repeat. Listen to the words you allow to ring in your memory. Read the words and know they can apply to your daily experiences. Observe how you go to sleep at night and see yourself greet the morning. In those ways you will see your beliefs play out.

Your doctrine is the liturgy of your day: it is read from the pulpit of the dawn and published in the parish pews of the paths you walk and the roads you drive. It is the light that shines and is both practical and practice-able. The intentions you hold define your days and your life. What are your intentions and how do they look in your daily life?

Promises to myself

If I were a mechanical vehicle, this would be my tune-up. The periodic practice of making and keeping promises to myself keeps me connected to the things that make me healthier and, therefore, better able to serve myself and others. I most frequently follow this daily promise-making process for forty days. When a friend of mine, the author Dr. Deanna Davis, asked what the motivation was behind choosing forty days, I laughingly confessed, "I know that experts say it takes twenty-one to instill a habit. It seemed to me twenty-one days wasn't long enough to reinforce the practice. And I'd just been talking to someone about the narrative of Noah's Ark. Forty days. Cooped up on a boat. I figured if Noah and all the animals could sustain forty days like that, I could sustain the practice of making, recording, and observing promises to myself on a daily basis. Not exactly a scientific formula but one that works for me and the participants I've guided on the process."

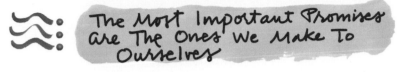

The Most Important Promises Are The Ones We Make To Ourselves

Friendship with oneself is all-important, because without it one cannot be friends with anyone else in the world.

—Eleanor Roosevelt

Eleanor is speaking of being kind to yourself. I extend that to encompass making and keeping promises to yourself. Your personal assessment of your own life has the greatest significance and impact. The appraisal of another only has the importance that is attributed to it. We can value the opinions and judgments of others without being determined or deterred by them. And we can be heartened by the intention of a promise extended without being disappointed when the promise is not fulfilled. Essentially, the most important promises are the ones we make to ourselves. Love yourself and fulfill those promises first.

 ## What Benefits are There...

The promises we make to ourselves are the things that assure us we have the capacity to keep our promises to others. I see a model for success in making promises. That which we speak out loud and promise to another is more likely to be acted upon than something we promise and simply keep to ourselves. Be forthcoming and bold and state your promise to a larger audience than just you. Create an environment of accountability so you learn to identify how it feels to make and keep a promise to yourself. Also, if you respond best to specifics, then be as specific as possible. If you know that you work better in the realm of ambiguity, then make the promise general and see what it helps you discover in the day. In each chapter, I offer a series of promises. Perhaps they will inspire you to create a set of your own.

What Is The Structure...

As I followed this promise-making process for forty consecutive days, I did not look back until I completed the forty days. Only when the process was finished did I review what I had written. Essentially, this practice is modeled on something that I guide others through: the Radmacher Focus Phrase process. If you would like to try this yourself, here is the model I teach:

1. A two-word (or very brief) prompt to remind me easily of the promise to myself throughout my day. Like this: Enthusiastic perseverance. I may include my own statements or others' thoughts/quotes that support or reinforce the fulfillment of the promise.

2. A brief statement supporting what I mean by the caption, always beginning with the two words, "I promise . . . to work through the 'much' to get to the 'must.'"

3. A statement actually making the Promise to Myself, framed in the same way I would say it if I were speaking to someone else. "Mary Anne, be specific and seize the zip and pizzazz you need to finish your tasks."

4. Looking ahead into TODAY—that means bringing the promise, with practicality, into my day. Like this: Create accountability for completing targeted processes including

a reward, use music and positive nutritional intake to boost your energy. This is essentially a brief exploration of ways that I might keep that promise to myself throughout the day.

Most evenings I reflected on the experience of that day. I would never write more than three short paragraphs. Taking note of how focusing on the two-word caption and the support material impacted my actions or decisions and if it made my day any richer or closer to one or more of my intentions. Many days it had a profound impact. Really, most days it had impact.

At the end of forty consecutive days, I was somewhat surprised to discover an amazing thread of consistency. You can see these promises featured throughout my intentions, the chapters of this book. Without consciously trying to achieve this, I drew out, in almost even balance, elements that matched the ten core intentional elements of my life.

Live With Intention

Many things in your day will capture your attention, but only a few will resonate with the aspirations of your heart. Pay attention to the ones that do. I want you to write. I want you to have the courage to pick up an instrument and correspond with yourself. Compose a very personal letter describing the surprising discoveries of your day. I want you to write because you know so much more than you think you know. If you are willing to learn, you will teach yourself to focus, to observe the details in your day that will instruct you. In this willingness to observe you will find that everywhere is a schoolroom and every moment is an opportunity to grow.

Today let your heart inform your eyes. Follow your intentions, in bliss, knowing that what bits, actions, and thoughts capture your eyes are in alignment with your heart, your purpose. As if you were a raven and the tasks of consequence were all the shiny, pretty things. Very satisfying.

Review your "Master List of Tasks" (I call mine "mind pour of stuff to do," but sometimes I play with calling the list "get to's" instead of "to do's"). Be amazed at the number of actions and results you've accomplished recently. All items in cadence with the intentions of your heart. Throughout the day, check on the compatibility of the action—is it engaged in with your greater view? In harmony? Flow? Ease?

When things didn't show up or were resistant, were you able to change course? Your eyes can confirm immediately when there is a disconnect, so when your eyes do not immediately confirm a disconnect, something out of kilter in your life eventually points to it. These measures begin to come naturally when you are utterly connected to your own intentions.

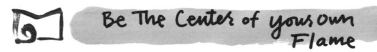

Be The Center of your own Flame

Tell your own story. Look to your deep knowing to validate your instincts. Look to others for learning, yes, but it is your own story you tell by the actions of your day. In fact, more largely, we tell the tale of our lives by the stories we repeat in our days.

"Because I said" is what your inner parent says to the equally inner child and then patiently explains the way/why of it. It is not because of someone else's road but because of what happens at your own intersection of insight—where experience, observation, instinct, and gathered knowledge come together and produce personal insight.

Clarity visits and often leaves no fingerprints, only sparkle.

 ## Invest in Consistent Measure

Goldilocks taught me a lot about evaluating consistent measure. Too Hot. Too Cold. Just Right.

Just right. The bandwidth that underscores virtually everything that is balanced with an "Ahhhhhh. Just right." It's the wireless signal with full bars. When I invest in consistent measure, I choose conscious observing of the "too" in my action. In an exchange with a client—too harsh, too gentle. In planning a dinner party—too many guests, too little food. In considering an opportunity for disagreement with my spouse—too personalized, too distant. Act on the identified, most significant priorities. Attribute measurable, specific aims to your entire day and let the sparkly distractions fly by.

Easy familiarity with your own intentions becomes a natural measure for virtually everything. It provides the basis for all the choices and commitments you make. Here is a set of questions that keeps me in balance with the "too" of my actions. If they make sense to you, they can become the three questions by which you can measure your decisions:

> *Increase—does it add value?*
> *Improve—does it improve quality?*
> *Impact—does it have consequence on my list of intentions?*

The greatest Risk in life is never Taking One

My dad used to tell me laughingly that on some mornings just climbing out of bed can be an act of courage. Am I fearless? No, hardly. I wrestle frequently with the seemingly uninvited visitor of fear. Unanswered, inexplicable medical issues raised fear within me. I went through a period of time in which I became increasingly ill. The cause was elusive, and no remedy seemed available. I stepped out of the grip of fear and started exploring.

Guessing. Risking new things. Quitting old patterns. It worked. The risks paid off immediately and my health continues to improve. In large part, the whole of my life has been a risk. Absent safety in my home life (in my childhood), my ventures outside were all risks. Starting a business. Expansion. Shrinking. Expansion without a safety net. Bankruptcy. Starting again. It was worth it. All of it. I hold no regret. How could I regret any of it? I love where I stand today, and it stands to reason that I cannot regret all the ways of risk that brought me to this very place.

Every possibility, each opportunity can stand at the threshold with the companion question "What if?"

Risk has been the best response to that question time and again. Certainty is an inner coach whispering in my ear, saying, "You'll never know unless you try." Being closely acquainted with the intentions of your life makes risk more palatable. When you assess the possibility before you and see the ways it aligns with your intention, it is easier to take the first step. And the steps that come after.

Psssst. Go ahead, make a promise to yourself. Risk it.

Those who dare to fail miserably can achieve greatly.
—John F. Kennedy

A pendulum swings. It's a law of physics. Equal and opposite reactions. Perhaps said more truthfully for my experience, each great success mustn't be partnered with an equally great failure. Perhaps the real partner in the equation is the willingness to fail on the way to achievement. The willingness to walk that road reveals another way, shines a light on another path. Willingness, sometimes called risk, accompanies the finest outreach. And that outreach is rewarded by connecting, daily, with your own intentions.

chapter 1

Completion

walk to the edge

Except for the folks who adhere to the leap-and-the-net-will-appear philosophy, the edge is a completion. When you arrive at the edge, there is no more land to walk. And if completion is a destination, there's one imperative that must be followed: just begin it.

Just Begin It

My skill set is not a rigid, contained metal box of tools but rather a glowing, expanding, contracting, breathing well of cosmic abilities that expands with my willingness to breathe more deeply and dig in. To any task. Any little task. I take advantage of my ability to see how a large thing is constructed of many small things. And I allow myself the thrill and the freedom of completing one small thing in the context of the large. That's what I mean by "Just begin it." In most days, there is more "do" than "day!" But working in small bits toward the larger completion, ultimately, gets a large thing done.

The most difficult aspect to amazing, creative productivity is the very first action: pick up what you need and begin.

Ideas and opportunities and "to do's" occasionally feel like the flock of birds in that classic Hitchcock horror flick, *The Birds*. Menacing. Dangerous, and threatening to land on your head at any moment. The vision of completion scatters them like a gust of wind and leaves just one. One bird—not so scary. One creative idea. One small task. Then all that remains is to begin. No prevaricating. No excuses and no anxiety.

Something that Pablo Picasso once asked has stayed with me. He wondered if an artist knew in advance exactly how and what they were going to create, why would they even bother creating it? Much of the pleasure of beginning and continuing a task lies in the pleasure of discovery. And discovery requires simply this: that you begin.

 ## Begin as If you Intend to Finish

See a friend. Walk in a garden. Take a deep breath. Try something new. Go a new way. Find out the name of a tree in your neighborhood. Plant a tree if there isn't one. Greet a stranger. Plant seeds. Watch the weather. Wait. Believe. Make a gift. Post a card. Give a smile. Offer to help. Appreciate a soldier. Play with a puppy. Stand in the wind. Walk up a hill. Stretch. Wonder. Imagine. Clean your closet. Use a different color pen. Use crayons. Dance. Sing a little song. Do the unexpected. Be extraordinary. Say yes to most things. Pretend it's easy. Say you're sorry. Use a new spice. Laugh loudest. Be extraordinary. Try it. Write something. Be original. Be well. Practice. Hop. Skip. Jump. Kiss somebody. Be special. Imagine something. Tell a story. Listen. Inspire. Be inspired. Swell with pride. Brag. Rearrange. Drive somewhere. Walk somewhere. Send a card. Visit a friend. Eat an apple. Be grateful. Go ahead and weep for this never-to-be-seen-again moment. Love as deeply as you can.

The real point of a thing is to begin it. And begin it with, at least, the ending, the finish, in mind. It does not mean you must finish at the moment. Nor does it mean that you must hold the specifics of what the finish will look like. One thing is certain: if you do not begin, you will never finish!

So to you, I say, "March along. Sing your song, either quietly or at the top of your lungs. Don't succumb to the tyranny of immediacy. Just do what you can . . . and recognize that many days the assessment of 'pretty darn good' ranks right up there with 'practically perfect.' Look in the mirror and remind yourself that you rock. And while you're doing the reminding, remind yourself that several successive 'starts' put you that much closer to the finish."

Call Them Targeted Completion Dates

Dead Line. DEADLINE. Just mouthing the words sounds ominous. The history of this word claims 1864 as its first appearance in the written record. This jibes with what I recall about it originating during the American Civil War: Prisoners were seldom held in purpose-built jails. More often, they were herded at gunpoint inside a makeshift boundary. The boundary had two lines, and the prisoner who stepped outside the inner boundary was ordered back, but one who overstepped the outer boundary was shot. Thus it was called the deadline.

I've long been discomforted inviting this word into my experience. In my quest for completion, I have determined that I no longer refer to deadlines. I call them "targeted completion dates." Unless the project truly has the dire consequence of death if it is not met, I'm not going to contribute to my general anxiety by referring to deadlines. More reflective of the truth of my life is a targeted completion date. I aim to reach my target! If my aim misses? I reset the target (negotiate or renegotiate) and aim again.

The Long-Term Done Lives in Today's Do

Love is the only force capable of transforming an enemy to a friend.

—Dr. Martin Luther King Jr.

I spent a day focused on these words of Dr. King. Throughout my day these words challenged me to love the many drivers I encountered behaving badly. One car had parked itself in the driving lane. The passenger was obviously taking down information from a "for rent" sign. I cautiously drove around them, instead of honking or shaking a shaming finger. MLK's admonishing phrase kept my road responses rooted in love instead of harshness.

How about taxes? The IRS. Yes. At this point in my exchange with taxes and the requisite accounting, I could consider them an enemy of sorts. The final, most arduous task, annual taxes, remains to be done. Perpetually put off, loathed. Just like an enemy. Well. Would love work with this, I wondered at the start of the day. If this was something I really loved doing, I'd use my best tools, in the most inviting environment, and I'd long to spend as much time as possible in the process. So I tried it. I pulled out sheets of my best paper. I got my favorite, easiest to use calculator. I set myself up in a room with a view. There was good light. I set out my best pens. I turned on my favorite music. And whoosh, off I went on this grand experiment inspired by Dr. King's words.

In this experiment I am artist in the land of figures, numbers, and columns. I thought about the professionals in the world who spend the bulk of their time in this way. This way that I have treated like an enemy. I extend love and appreciation to them and open my possibility to associating with them to manage this process that I do not naturally embrace. I used the model of working in love and using small segments toward completing the whole. And I did "walk to the edge" and complete the process. Surprisingly, in good shape and time.

Today I have extended the force of love, and there has been a transformation. I know, because yesterday an onerous task awaited me. And today I have completed what was a dreaded chore. A shift in perspective and a little bit of "do" arrived, almost painlessly, at "done!" At the end of the matter, I felt transformed in my own view. That is, of course, where Dr. King understood is the only place that transformation can occur.

> **Today I have extended the force of love, and there has been a transformation.**

 ## Lead or Follow a leader

I am the leader in my own day. Even when I have worked for other people, I have put myself in charge of my day, my time, and my accountability. On the best and most productive day, I am able to follow this instruction: "Take a deep breath and do the difficult thing first." When I do that, all things in the remainder of the day feel like a game. Really.

Winged Thoughts

Ordinary people are compelled by the extraordinary; extraordinary people are engaged by the ordinary.

Actions are mirrors of remembering. Perspective is the harmony to the lyric actions of life.

I am grateful to work independently and swim without resistance in the sea of my own creativity.

I govern no priorities but my own.

Great leadership is not the visit of an unexpected fate but rather a flame that is kept burning in spite of risk and opposition.

Appreciate the practiced pause.

Anger is often a masquerade of insecurity and personal uncertainty.

Irritation rises from the belief that things must be a specific way.

The momentum to fulfill a promise comes easily once the decision to make the promise is complete.

Speaking the truth is harder before you do it—afterward, it is pure relief.

Invest yourself wholly in matters of consequence; do not become absorbed by the trivial.

Dispense efficiently with the perfunctory and move to the planned and purposeful: allow for alchemy.

 Winged Thoughts

Be a servant to your craft.

Recognize equal value in building and deconstructing.

Follow the creative impulse to innovation.

Pursue the natural progression toward unknown form.

Perform an action with the expectation of creating different results. Therefore the action must be different.

Allow your intentions their practical application in the day; and be encouraged, in the large, by your intentions, not discouraged, in the small, by disappointments.

Tend to a few things well (not "too many" things, quickly).

It's easier to see when you are not moving at warp speed.

Engaged observation is the gift of the even pace.

Allow "good enough" to seem like perfection.

Stepping aside from habit makes room for fresh winds of power.

Manage the much and stay connected to the must of your own choices.

Peak experiences of life become jewels that you wear proudly, and they sparkle and shine to cast light on your path.

Winged Thoughts

Word Birds

Is there any better accompaniment to the business of morning than the enveloping bass of the foghorn?

The day is up for grabs before the ink dries on the to-do list.

Maintain a simple cadence. Even in a complex orchestration, the most accomplished musician plays a piece a note at a time.

Let imagined outcomes drive chosen actions.

The admonition to love yourself precedes any effort at effectiveness.

Diligently work toward the completion of promises.

With the pressure of the calendar behind you, your day evolves into its destiny.

We savor our distractions; they keep us from the weight of our greatness.

Poor planning changes everyone's priorities.

All you're doing today is swimming in a sea of your choices.

Interview well in your day and you'll hear, "You're highered."

Speculation is unfruitful. So today, this moment, there is sun. There is work to be done and your own road to pursue.

 Winged Thoughts

Remember the balance—this action is the now and its consequence lives forever. Your efforts find purchase in the soil of your future.

Leverage opportunity and seize joy.

Tea, please, with the distractions served on the side.

Possess an extraordinary talent for helping others see the world differently.

Being alive is a fierce responsibility.

If I had to paint it, what would the colors in the landscape of my heart be?

Raise me up high above all these details—from above I see the glorious pattern. Knee deep in details, I see only that which must be done next.

Busy-ness is the validation of small minds.

Call them targeted completion dates rather than deadlines.

Leverage opportunity and seize joy.

When creating a plan: listen and hear opportunity; seize specifics and absorb generalities; invite innovation; be willing to imagine.

Promises to Myself • • • • •

If you experience a sense of being overwhelmed at the number of targeted completion dates that appear on your current calendar, you might try applying these promises to yourself.

Utmost Priority

Friends trump almost everything.

—mar

• I promise to act on my identified, most significant priorities.

• "Attribute measurable, specific aims to your entire day and let the sparkly distractions fly by."

• Looking into this day, this might mean—be flexible; remain undeterred by distraction; use the hourglass to time focus on a project; restore and renew throughout the day with water, stretching, and music.

Keen Focus

I like the fact that listen *is an anagram of* silent . . .

—Alfred Brendel

• I promise to listen and act upon my mission and passion.
• "Connect, in practical, visible terms, to what you are called to be."
• Looking into my day, this might mean—fresh eyes and tuned ears, recreating the way I teach, letting go of the small in favor of the large (holiday cards might turn into new year's greetings, dear friends).

Just Breathe

If I'm not on fire, it's not urgent.

—mar

• I promise to turn down the volume on the pending demands. "Do one thing and do your best."

• TODAY—live with the grace of the small (one thing, okay, maybe two . . .), not the overwhelming beauty of the large (all things at once); discover one thing at a time; be in accord with your own tempo—turn on your music.

Engage Excellence

Excellence in any pursuit is the late, ripe fruit of toil.

—W.M.L. Jay

• I promise to focus on quality not quantity.

• "Tend a few things well (not too many things, quickly)."

• Looking into my day, this might mean—just one artful project at the festival, being totally attentive to conversation, packaging cookies for friends with excellent details not just efficiency.

leverage opportunity and seize joy.

Enthusiastic Perseverance

In the realm of ideas, everything depends on enthusiasm.
In the real world, all rests on perseverance.

—Johann Wolfgang von Goethe

- I promise to work through the "much" to get to the "must."
- "Be specific and seize the zip and pizzazz to finish your tasks."
- TODAY—work off a detailed list; create accountability for completing targeted processes; use music and positive nutritional intake to boost your energy.

Friends are the utmost of all priorities.

—mar

Strong people have strong weaknesses.

—Peter Drucker

You are lost the instant you know what the result will be.

—Juan Gris

There are two kinds of light—the glow that illumines
and the glare that obscures.

—James Thurber

Just
Breathe

chapter 2

Spirit

listen hard

 ## In Listening to others, I Can Hear the Universe

A person hears only what they understand.

—Johann Wolfgang von Goethe

A familiar refrain begins many arguments, "But I told you . . ."

"You did not."

"Yes! Three times."

"You did?"

"Yes, I explained to you three different times."

"I must not have heard you."

"You heard me, all right. You just didn't understand. Why didn't you tell me you didn't understand?"

That's a good question. Goethe was so clear. We only readily hear what we already understand. That makes it hard to tell someone when I do not understand. I'm not exactly certain, in the moment that I don't. This is why it is erroneously said you can't teach an old dog new tricks. The first and really only new trick an old dog needs to learn is how to listen hard and well.

I've seen Goethe's observation at work in so many ways. Remember when any adult spoke in cartoonist Charles Schultz's imagined world of the *Peanuts* comic strip? We never knew what the grownups were really saying because we were only treated to what the child heard, which was a rapid succession of, "Mwah, mwah, mwah, mwah."

Focusing on this phrase informed me how many times I heard words but did not understand them. I have developed a couple of different habits that have served me well. Often I flatly confess that I am unclear on what was just said. Sometimes I am able to say, "Would you say that to me another way?" These two responses have allowed me to inform myself that I was not grasping the message and give myself another chance to understand.

> Being willing to see the divine in others completely changes my exerience.

Really, in learning to listen hard and invite new patterns into my old ways, I lean against the wall of uncertainty and am able to whisper, "This one thing I know for certain . . . I want to understand." The real prayer is for open eyes—eyes that are able to see the signs that are always there.

Hearing. What about seeing? They make effective partners. Being willing to see the divine in others completely changes my experience. It is rightly said that we see what we are looking for. In the sense of heightened awareness of the divine in others, not only am I more inclined to see, but my own divine nature also becomes more visible. On days that I practice listening hard and seeing the divine in others, nothing really transforms in the actual day itself. And yet all things are different. Wanting to see the finest in others lifts back a curtain on the stage of life. What a show begins. There are unexpected driving courtesies, tender moments in the middle of the grocery store, opportunities to serve and be served. When I issue the invitation to see the divine in others, everyone seems to respond with an enthusiastic, "Yes, here I am." It's an invitation that calls to mind the Unicorn speaking to Alice in Wonderland, "I'll believe in you if you'll believe in me."

In the realm of spirit, it takes a synergy far beyond just hearing and seeing to consider God. God is not containable. In the instant someone declares, "Aha, God is *this*!" God appears as something unexpected. Beyond definition or immediate grasp, God is the ultimate magic show of the universe. There God goes, "Watch me pull a rabbit out of my hat. Presto!" Oooooh. What a rabbit it is.

In Spite of Pain, We Know

In joy, in sorrow, in pain, in understanding, in perplexity, in how we rise up and in the manner we fall down, in how we can see our reflection and in how we cannot conceive of how we are or how the world is, when things seem in order and when things appear chaotic—in all these walks and ways we know there is a universal force that supports our breath. In spite of anything and because of everything, we know. And we remember to listen.

That universal force isn't always sweet and considerate. The still small voice prefers not to rise to crescendo in order to be heard. Of course, sometimes it resorts to some whoop ass, but only in extreme circumstances—and only when I'm really not paying attention.

Seen or Unseen, a World Exists Beside Me

Pay attention to the synchronicity of the events in your life. As an example, the day after my doctor said I was "running on fumes," my car was out of gas in the driveway. People have many different names for those visiting signals, the signs, the synergies of our lives. There was a magic carpet ride I took when I was young. In awe, I said "Yes!" to God. And in unique and personal ways, I have been saying yes ever since. Yes to the awe and yes to God.

The patterns, the visual unlikelihood, the stretch of imagination asking, "A piece of flat paper did that?" The interconnectedness of the origami folds strikes me as symbolic of the complex layers and folds of our days. Crease, fold, harsh straight line, each flat fold building upon flat fold until shaken or the strength of breath is applied. With breath or stretch, there is magic. Form recognized. What was flat, unfamiliar, becomes a bird in flight. This calls to mind those "aha" moments—when all the murky, disconnected complexities line up in magnificent order to say, "This is the lesson I have been creating for you. This is a lasting, difficult beauty for your life."

In the Practiced Pause, You Can Learn to Listen

Racers at the starting line are poised, positioned to surge forward at the sound of the starting gun. Sometimes I am like that in conversation. So excited about a thought I have, I become ready, positioned to speak. The "starting gun" becomes the first perceptible pause in the other person's statements. Jump. Start. Seize the single opportunity to get my sentences in. But have I listened? Did I hear the last half of what was said? No. Not really. Hardly at all.

When I really listen hard, I take notes, either literally or in my mind. I write things down as someone is speaking and allow those written prompts to remind me, later, of something I want to say or share. When I take notes, I speak much less. When I pause my talking habit and really listen to what the other person is saying, I see that I am more likely to ask questions than to make statements. A conversation becomes less a game of my turn, now your turn, and more a collaborative effort to create something greater than our individual stated thoughts. It's a lot like two bakers agreeing to work together to produce a healthy, yummy loaf of bread that will, in turn, nourish not only themselves but others as well.

There are so many different ways to listen and things to listen to. It is said that music is made as much of the silences between the notes as of the notes themselves. So it must be in this process of learning to listen. The spaces in between, the practiced pause, contribute in a profound way to the process of listening. Do we listen to "spirit" any differently than we listen to our friends? I think all these ways contribute to successful listening. Auditory. Memory. Anatomy. Intuition. Tactile. Experience. Emotion. Observing my own habits in listening improves them. I am continually amazed that after so much effort to improve my listening skills, I still interrupt people, still jump to "have my turn." It takes a lot of practice to learn the pause, to be in the space between the notes.

We must be both gentle and fierce.

Winged Thoughts

Meeting the unexpected with love is the ultimate perspective.

How sweet on the tongue is the well-spoken word.

I am most successful finding what I am looking for when I don't know what it is. Listen to intuition and connect the dots between everything you know.

We admire most in others the qualities we most long for in ourselves: just as that of which we are most critical in others is that which we dislike most in ourselves.

The world itself plays a symphony for me if I will only listen.

"Do you believe in prayer?" she asked. Quietly, my heart answered, "My entire life is a prayer. I am a prayer." I smiled and assured her, "Yes, I believe."

Anyone who's ever planted a seed and later bit into a red juicy tomato knows, at least, to wonder and, at best, to believe in miracles.

Things appear to transform you in their own, ineffable time.

Participate in unpolished directness, observation, and truthfulness.

From many roads—merges one road.

Tales are written on the unfolding scroll of vision, and laughter with the ink of adventure and the pen of commitment.

Word Birds

Instinct sometimes masquerades as impulse.

Pick up and see, again, what it is that constitutes your strength.

There's a place for the quiet and neutral. In the context of things that are more complex, neutrality plays well with others.

Talk about the transferable skills of the spirit . . . if this is true within me, then this is true outside of me. It could also be called living from the metaphor.

I am living the fire.

History grows our expectations and roots our beliefs in spite of us.

I am willing to listen more and speak less.

I am willing to listen to a friend's problem and not be compelled to create a solution.

I am willing to be who I am in full measure.

I am willing to transition from "just barely" to "fully and unreservedly."

Everyone's flame (light) feeds the fire of life.

I move my pen to the ever-changing rhythms of my spirit.

Fully express core gifts in a consistent, powerful, impacting way.

Winged Thoughts

Punctuate the large with the many joyful smalls . . . take verve and power from the enormity of what is before you.

Manifestation: continue to connect to universal, spiritual practices intuitively and without fanfare; continue to improve the conditions of your life by facing your patterns with compassion.

The first good of compassion we can know is what it does to our own soul.

Epiphany exists beyond the realm of reason.

By sharing my space, a greater space is created. In sharing my love, a greater love is created. In extending any true thing with authenticity, it is enlarged.

Being willing to see the divine in everyone changes the day. Willingness is an engraved spiritual invitation to receive the very thing we are willing and receptive to.

I am accountable to the promise I have made in love.

Let my own listening be acute.

Relax into the natural embrace of the day and enjoy the gifts that come.

What is essesntial we recognize with the breath of our own spirit.

Seen or unseen, there are worlds that exist alongside my own.

Create a new path of seeing with simple compassion.

This day. Each day is a mountain of unknowable mystery.

If you pay attention to all the messages that you "learned through," you have constructed the fundamental curriculum of your spirit.

Listen hard, like a conductor evaluating each note of a new orchestration. Each note contributes to the impact of the whole. Master hearing the whole to understand the parts.

Poetry sings the tune without the words—live your life today as if you were the poetry.

When it's the right kind of risk, people fly and don't fall. And, well, if they do fall, they don't stay bruised for long.

I can have ease in spite of having no control over others or the environment. Perhaps because of it . . .

Listen. Hear opportunity. Seize specifics and absorb the general. Create a simple, affordable, extraordinary plan to launch your dreams on a daily basis. What thing will you do to awaken your spirit today?

The miraculous and the non-miraculous have synthesized into a wondrous, single entity that I embrace as my life.

Finishing what is necessary, we go on not with fire but with warmth and in the absence of fear. We must be both gentle and fierce.

Promises to Myself • • • • •

Do you often give thought to things beyond your own explanation? Do you wonder about the power of coincidence and things greater than your own knowing? Perhaps you can listen more deeply to your own promise by applying some of these promises to your days.

Word Power

Your word is your wand.
—Florence Scovel Shinn

• I promise to be connected to the impact of my word(s).

• "Your core is reflected in the mirror of your words."

• TODAY—speak with intention and precision; call the good forward with yes, and set aside how and what if for the day; listen more and speak less.

Open Heart

Remember me. I will remember you.
—The Qur'an (2:152)

• I promise to be at the door of my heart all day.

• "Operate close to the angels today and be strong in your open heart."

• TODAY—be generous with your praise; be willing to welcome new souls into your circle; see others with your divine glasses on and observe God in all.

Reciprocal graces

An outward and visible sign of an inward and spiritual grace.
—The Book of Common Prayer

- I promise to be gentle with myself and others.
- "Just hold the quiet in your heart and listen."
- TODAY—flow; tend essential things; accept when graces are extended, offer them when you can . . . and ask for what you need.

Inspired Listening

I became silent and began to listen.
I discovered, in the silence, the voice of God.
—Søren Kierkegaard

- I promise to follow the divine whisper of possibility. "Still the sounds around you in order to hear what's essential."
- TODAY—be open to all solutions; act on the impulses of your spirit; pray; consider silence an appropriate means of communication.

chapter 3

Health

practice wellness

 ### Self-Care: Movement Toward Health

Henry Ford said, "Chop your own wood and it will warm you twice." Though the obvious connection to wellness is seen in the cardiovascular benefit of this action, I perceive the meaning to be: Take care of yourself first. Many consider altruism the hallmark of an elevated soul. Giving primary care to yourself, first, is not only practical, it is also essential. Individuals trained in the liturgy of self-sacrifice and denial have difficulty seeing the balance between self-care and self-indulgence. In an objective glance, they appear quite different.

Self-care tends to the fundamental requirements of a healthy and contented life. A healthy person will choose the comfort and ease of another person above their own, periodically but not consistently. If daily bread is a metaphor for all essentials, then if you feed your whole baguette to someone with great frequency, you become a need for someone else to fill. The factor of generosity, so rewarding in a healthy lifestyle, can become self-indulgence. The conventional grasp of this phrase involves giving too much to yourself. I'm mirroring that understanding here. Suggesting it can be that peculiar thing that masquerades as martyrdom. Generosity turned to indulgently giving too much. Giving to the detriment of your own values and needs. "I've given so much. How could they treat me this way? I've given everything I had. I'm all poured out." One must ask, "Who is doing the pouring?"

That Henry Ford phrase addresses the basic message of self-reliance. Providing your own essential needs empowers you to care not only for yourself, but for others as well. Tending watchfully to your requirements builds a resource base that allows for positive generosity (thus "warming twice"). *Generosity* and *(re)generative* share a Latin root, meaning, among other things, "magnanimous" or "to create." Regenerating is restoring what was spent. Generating is the process of creating what previously did not exist. As a generous soul, I grasp the impulse to "give it all away." Consider a sourdough baguette. Sourdough starter generously recreates itself as long as some portion is retained upon which the rebuilding of the starter is based.

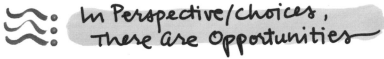

In Perspective/choices, There are Opportunities

Perspective's a funny thing. As challenging as my own experience may seem, there is always someone "who's got it worse than I do." Here's what I know: "There are starving children in Ethiopia" did nothing to help me eat the ubiquitous tomato aspic that found its way to a waiting, trembling platter of iceberg lettuce at so many of my childhood meals. I was willing to send as much of that aspic to those hungry children as I might pack. From my limited understanding of the postal system and relative worldwide distances, I just wasn't sure that aspic would travel all that well.

My point?

Comparison of our own pain to the pain of others is an ineffective tool. My pain is my pain. Period. The pain is not lessened by recognizing that someone else's pain seems more complex than mine.

I find that such comparisons only invite my inner Drill Master to appear and start barking at me, "C'mon along, wimpy little soldier, there are others who bear up so much better than you!"

Comparison simply serves as an override button to disregard my own best interests and plough through the pain. That's what almost did me in one spring. When I got bronchitis, I told myself that it wasn't as bad as last year. Then it moved into pneumonia, and I said that I didn't feel as poorly as I imagined pneumonia to feel. "It's not that bad. It's not as bad as

> Comparison of our own pain to the pain of others is an ineffective tool.

_____ (this is where you fill in an appropriate kind of comparison)."

Rubbish, I say. It's all just dressed-up denial. Denial going to a masquerade party as noble suffering and inappropriate overextending. I should have compassion. For all. And in my best five-year-old voice, hear me squeak, "Me first." Yes indeed. Compassionate care for ourselves needs a higher rank in our days.

What an ongoing life lesson it is for me to understand that my profound service to others must (and always) begin with service to myself.

May I have the fortitude to see and serve my own needs first, today, that I might fully and uncompromisingly fulfill my vision of service to others. In fact, to greet the day in this way:

Dear Day: I greet you with ease and rising wellness. I invite you to shepherd the right people into all my spaces. In all my ventures let me be reminded that they are first spiritual adventures before they are any other kind of venture. In all your elements I am a willing student and teacher, both. I am content to be both magician and muse. I embrace each choice as an

opportunity to measure the action against my own intentions. I
anticipate a consistent energy on all your paths, and at the end of
you, I suspect sleep will come upon me sweetly. Glad you're here.
—love, Me.

 ## Choose Love

When my dad was first reviewing road safety with me, his fifteen-year-old, bearing-a-driver's-permit daughter, he narrated a specific circumstance with a phrase I've often repeated in my mind.

A car jumped its turn at a four-way stop . . .

"You could have gone—it was your turn—but then that car would have barreled into you. You would have been right, sis, but dead-right."

He also observed in similar circumstances, "You can choose to be right or alive."

Along the way, this driving instruction has been co-opted into a greater spiritual teaching. Aptly applied to our cooperative journey on the roads of daily experience—"You can be right or be happy."

When I recognize my many choices, I often encourage myself with two words—"Choose love." When criticism would get a laugh but hurt some feelings, when a warned-of event comes to pass and "I told you so" is allowable, when directions are asked to be repeated (not listened to the first time)—in so many opportunities for chatter and chastisement—choose love. What builds up positive, loving choice? The conscious effort of choosing love over more judgmental options, rather than offering annoyed correction—love becomes the basis for sound assessment. Love is an excellent measure in all choices. Wellness is based in many such sound measures: moderation, caution, information, balance.

Turn Yourself Toward a Regular Sabbath

Sabbath. It is defined as a period of rest. A set-aside time unique in that it is both away from what is usual and dedicated to something that is not usual, most often identified as rest, study, or prayer. It is usually one day of turning from one thing and turning to something else. The extended sabbatical implies a leave from ordinary experiences for a defined period of time. To sabbatize is to observe a single day of set-aside "Sabbath moments." Taking a sabbatical can be a condensed discipline in perspective, an exercise of turning from that which is undesirable and turning, perhaps with a prayerful understanding, to a better way of being.

Beyond Desire, Move Into Admire

The secret of happiness is to admire without desiring.

—Francis H. Bradley

Much of what I ate seemed healthy and nutritionally sound. And then there was cream in my coffee, cheese (on and in and around everything), wheat of any sort, and eggs. All these foods are exceptionally beneficial and appealing—just not in the balance I consumed them and, turns out, not for my body.

To understand the severe switch I made in my nutritional intake, you need to know that my honorary title was "butter queen" and that for many birthdays I have been served a pound of Irish butter on a cake platter. Now the impact of my transition to no dairy products should be clearer.

Perhaps there is a food you desire over any other. My favorite was butter. I could write quite a bit about its elegant function melting atop warm baked things and its superb performance as an ingredient. If my former cooking habits needed an advertising slogan, it would have to be "Everything's better with butter."

My nutritional changes were invited by a prolonged illness that culminated in severe pneumonia. It was almost accidental that I discovered at the core of my chronic health issues were challenges with specific types of food, among them butter. My passion for butter was almost legendary among my friends. So imagine their surprise when butter passed by me at the communal table and I had none. And I demonstrated no sign of remorse. My friends offered sympathy and plenty of commiserating phrases like "That's awful." I realized I understood the intention of Bradley's quote in this context. I admire this beautiful food and its cousins, cream and cheese. I do not desire them because today I desire my health and vitality more. Admiring a thing does not require me to acquire it. In a metaphysical way, in admiration I get the pleasure without the consequence. Will this always be true in practice? I don't know. It's true right now, and for right now, that's enough.

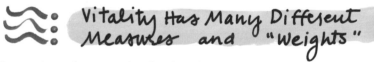

Vitality Has Many Different Measures and "Weights"

I experienced yet another landmark moment in this journey toward inspired living and vibrant health. My weight today matches what I have declared on my driver's license for many years. For the first time, it is correct. Accurate. The truth.

My journey toward health has never been about weight management. In sixth grade when my mother had to bump me to the ladies section of the department store to wear size 8 and 10 clothes, I recognized that I was "large" for my age. That has been true for as long as I can remember. Efforts to govern my weight have been painfully unsuccessful throughout my life. Of course, now I know it was because I was in continual metabolic crisis, eating food daily that brought allergic reaction and harm to my entire system.

The last time I listed my actual weight was at the time my first driver's license was issued, at sixteen years old. It was the first and last time I accurately reflected my weight. In the few times I've had to renew the content on my driver's license (a move, a renewal date that was not automatic), I have guessed or prevaricated. Which is a fancy way of saying, "I lied." Why? I can think of three reasons at least. The truth horrified me. I didn't know my actual weight because I'd long ago stopped stepping on scales or looking when a doctor required that I step on a scale. I was ever hopeful and willing to list what I imagined my weight might soon be.

One of the most significant differences between my previously imagined weight and my actual current weight is this: my objective in this journey was to be healthy and feel vibrant, strong, and energetic. In this recent effort at health management, I did not have weight loss as an objective. I had tried for so long to lose weight that it didn't occur to me that it was even a possibility. While I was unwilling to declare, in writing, the sum, the actual weight of my parts, at least I extended the love and acceptance to myself. I was grateful that round has always been my favorite shape!

With my attention on wellness, not weight loss, my body has been giving me its own answers, finding an equilibrium that involves less weight on my bones. To say "I feel as if a burden has been lifted" is a profound understatement. It's an understatement I will be happy to live with.

Today, three words in that sentence are truer than ever: Today I will live.

Winged Thoughts

Weariness readily overcomes vision. Weariness is ever poised, ready to overcome vision.

Punctuate your movement with stillness.

Absent hurry, many aspects of a fully occupied day become an invitation for unexpected joy, gift, and pleasure.

Every expression is a matter of choice.

Run all decisions through this filter: "Will this contribute to my physical well-being?"

Sourdough starter generously recreates itself as long as a portion is retained upon which the rebuilding is based.

A loving understanding of personal needs creates ease and a welcome that lasts a lifetime without resistance. As a willing and observant student, intuitive and dedicated, confidently build successful protocols based on what works for your personal best.

Change the vocabulary of your world by dwelling on what's gone right. What about the whole world?

Spirit turns performance into being. Rest after flying at high altitude ensures that the chronic call to speed, activity, and performance-based measures is balanced.

Courage both whispers and roars.

Clarity and compassion, pressed into service, overcome the forces of negativity.

Nonaction is a misnomer. See that not doing is essential to good work, positive health, healing, and appropriate doing.

It is called "somebody else's job" for a reason. There's freedom in accepting that the only job you should do is your own.

On a wearied little road, there is scant space for wide words.

Criticism of others is how self-loathing gets its exercise.

A fallow field is working toward a productive harvest— every (heart) harvest has its story of seemingly unproductive days.

A day off: naps punctuated by pleasures.

It's not malaise: it's the simmering of creative stew.

You are your own home. Home is an answer of place from deep within you.

The way you speak to yourself when no one else can hear dramatically impacts the way you speak to others when you can be heard.

Dance is the way the body spells, music is the way the soul speaks, conversation is the invitation for the mind to imagine.

If you can shout, you can sing. If you can stomp, you can dance. If you can accuse, you can incite. If you can run, you can race. If you can fear, you can imagine.

Promises to Myself • • • • •

Do you find yourself struggling with reoccurring health issues? Is your practice at wellness inconsistent? Consider spending some days making a promise to yourself that is centered on your own well-being.

Courageously Unconventional

It's an odd feeling though, writing against the current: difficult to entirely disregard the current. Yet, of course, I shall.
—Virginia Woolf

• I promise to behave/think outside habitual structures.

• "You are unlimited in your ability to be inventive."

• Looking into my day, this might mean—writing/working in bed instead of at my desk, asking for help when I'd do it myself, delivering different messages to friends, surprising the guests (and myself) at tonight's lecture.

Straight Scoop

When one is frank, one's very presence is a compliment.
—Marianne Moore

• I promise to participate in directness, observation, and truthfulness which stays unpolished.

• "Be forthcoming with the whole spectrum of what is true."

• Looking into this day, this might mean—not taking on additional projects, regardless of their merit; expressing responses, including anger, with integrity; having a solid yes or no along with my responses . . . very little "maybe."

Encourage Muscle

The finest gift you can give anyone is encouragement.
—Sidney Madwed

• I promise to strengthen myself in every way. "Confirm your strength(s) in every opportunity."

• TODAY—serve stamina in the physical and energetic realms; support your health in body and spirit in all your choices; practice wellness.

Environment Matters

We're too busy not to have order.
—Martha Stewart

• I promise to be attentive to my physical environment.

• "Look from the inside out and consider your immediate world a reflection in a mirror."

• TODAY—as you consider your imminent move, surround yourself with meaningful objects; if you can see it, it should be important; transition objects to places they will be happiest.

chapter 4

Play

play with abandon

Experts from diverse fields of research are weighing in on the broad benefits of play. When corporate problem solvers engage that playful part of their brains, they are discovering a different road to solutions. Play invites a different kind of thinking. What many years ago appeared edgy and avant-garde in corporate structure is beginning to be accepted as mainstream protocol. The playroom is no longer limited to primary schools and day-care centers. Play nurtures the body and spirit and gives a fresh wind to the occasionally closed mind.

 ## The Key to Brilliance is Serious: Play

Your life is a piece of music. It could be titled "Transition and Change." Some transitions are marked by event, celebration, gifts, symbolism. Others slip into our lives more quietly. *Mezzo piano*. Falling gently, leaves of the oak as they change color and flutter to the ground.

Today everything is possible until it isn't; today I have all I need; today is a celebration of any and all sorts—simply that I am alive. On a day absent so many of my dear ones, being alive is a fierce responsibility. It's not so much that I must live for them, live the life they cannot, but more that with the privilege of breath at waking, of putting my feet to the floor, comes a heightened sense of promise.

What will I do with everything that is possible in this day? Embrace the contradiction. The highways of life are not linear. The wide-open lanes of our days travel every which way, in all directions. Just get on the road and play.

Some Days are Simply Meant for Playing

Take something that another says personally or laugh. Make "something" of it or make light of it. Today I erred on the side of silliness, and I have many wonderful memories to prove it. This was a day I let my highly sensitive self have most of the day off. It was a day when I was willing to make light of almost everything. This drew out my inner comic, and was that ever a lot of fun. I had my friend, who was driving us to the store, laughing so hard she almost had to pull over to the side of the road for safety. Silliness: some days are simply meant for playing.

This phrase was a key element to what is now my "classic" body of work. I started my company with handmade greeting cards. And that was my vision. I love mail. I love writing to friends and sending things with a real stamp. Receiving mail makes any day almost a holiday. My commitment to meaningful greeting cards came naturally to me. Just as naturally as the longing for the water on a particular cerulean-blue-just-out-of-the-tube sky day in July on the coast of Oregon.

In the early years of my company, I was the all and everything. I staffed the retail/showroom space while I did all the production work for the wholesale element. It was a Saturday, and the earnestness of my posted retail hours and the obligation to fulfill the orders awaiting my hand were singing loudly. There was a larger message. It was the symphony of summer. My wet suit was in my closet at work. My boogie board was in my vehicle. I grabbed a discarded card prototype and wrote, by way of explanation for the closed door, "Some days are simply meant for playing." I taped it to the door and gleefully spent the remainder of my day playing in the sea. I returned to work the following day, refreshed and ready to produce! I was surprised to find five "orders" scooted under the door for the "poster" that was taped as a message to my visitors.

A day of play produced the product that would come to be the hallmark of my writing and the basis for a lifetime of satisfying work.

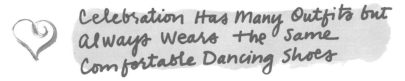

Celebration Has Many Outfits but always Wears the Same Comfortable Dancing Shoes

Hospitality and holiday need not be governed by a calendar. There are many reasons in the course of life that call for celebration. I am most happy when I am creating an event for no particular reason at all on a rather ordinary Thursday. Being grateful to be alive, having a memory that works or an arm that can spin in giant circles is enough of a reason to celebrate.

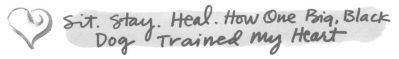

Sit. Stay. Heal. How One Big, Black Dog Trained My Heart

I was flying home after visiting my dearest friends: the family that had adopted my sweet Labrador retriever named Judah. A set of life circumstances had led to placing Judah in a home where he would have children to herd and a much greater opportunity for exercise and doing all the things that big dogs love to do. He was absolutely thrilled with his new family. And they loved having Judah as part of their pack.

My heart was very heavy as the plane began winging back to my own home. My visit had been to say good-bye to the dog that had taught me so much and had done such good work for two families. Judah was dying of lung cancer. I thought my grief would cry itself a river. Right there on the plane. My seatmate asked if I was all right, and all I could muster was, "My dog is dying." She understood immediately, patting my hand with the quiet compassion that understanding brings.

I started thinking about all the gifts of joy and play this amazing dog had brought into my life. And I decided to answer the void of my loss with a list of all the lessons that dog delivered to my heart. Even in my sorrow, Judah led me to focus on the good right in front, just as he naturally always did. So here's some of the list, as I made it, on that flight home. Though Judah did indeed leave the planet just days later, his lessons live on, and I will share a few of them with you. I've playfully titled them "Sit, Stay, Heal" because that is how Judah trained me and healed me over the years. Play wasn't the top of Judah's priority list, but it was very close.

Be clear on your priorities:
1) Food;
2) Treats;
3) See previous;
4) Rolling in the grass;
5) Playing with your pack and Yummies (see first and second).

Be fully engaged with the task in front of you.
When you're tired of running, just sit down.
When you're tired of turning in circles chasing your tail, stop.
When you have an itch, go to the best scratcher.

You really have to like someone to share your food with them.

The enthusiasm behind the tail is more important than the things the tail knocks over.

Engage in pleasures ravenously.

Even seemingly undesirable activities can be turned into adventure.

The risk of playing too hard and getting hurt is worth it if you're playing with a really cool dog. Play until you can't. Play, romp, bite, roll, sniff each other's butts, sit on each other, wrestle, run, rest. Repeat.

The present moment is where all the good stuff happens.

Play grows in the soil
of a cheerful heart.

Winged Thoughts

Allow fun to permeate the day.

Play grows in the soil of a cheerful heart.

Calculated mischief is invigorating.

Pick something outrageous just for practice.

Connect to the cadence of your natural stride.

Get the pleasure of a thing without the burden of the ownership.

Explore rather than expect.

In your heart—joy. At your table—abundance. In your home—peace.

You choose the music for the dance of the day.

Joy waits, an unopened package wrapped in ribbons, for dawn. Joy waits for the heart that says, "This must be a holiday—and this gift must be for me."

Promises to Myself · · · · ·

Play carries the impulse of being the reward at the end of a project. It is the proverbial carrot at the end of the stick. Including a daily promise to yourself to bring play into your day may teach you many other applications that play brings to your party.

get moving

Walking is the best possible exercise.
—Thomas Jefferson

• I promise to be purposely active today.

• "You're better at being focused and still when you also partner with playful movement."

• TODAY—crank the tunes and dance; bundle up and go for a walk; fidget; try two stairs at a time.

Play well

Work and play are words used for the same thing under differing conditions.
—Mark Twain

• I promise to have some fun!

• "Revel and roll around in each sweet aspect of your day like a Labrador in summer grass."

• TODAY—do what you love; wrap necessary tasks in love; be a little silly; seize the spirit of the holiday and hoist it to the joists of your soul.

Play gently

We do not cease to play because we grow old.
We grow old because we cease to play.
—George Bernard Shaw

- I promise to go easy in the day.
- "Punctuate your movement with stillness."
- TODAY—nap!; address that sense of weariness; have a short "list" or no list at all; play upon your impulse.

Fun Prevails

It isn't the great big pleasures that count the most;
it's making a great deal out of the little ones.
—Jean Webster

- I promise to allow fun to permeate the day.
- "You can have fun and make significant contributions to the world."
- Looking into my day, this might mean—insert fun _____ (here); setting up my festival booth in a cold barn turns into a festivity; do things with friends; get the music on; dance through ordinary activities.

The sum of the whole is this: walk and be happy; walk and be healthy.
—Charles Dickens

Get lost. That's the best way to find yourself.
—mar

when you're
tired of
running
just sit down.

gratitude
laugh

I hold gratitude deeply. It rumbles around in my soul, and it comes tumbling out as laughter. The capacity to experience gratitude in all circumstances is tied, experientially, to laughter and laughing. In moments when I am disconnected to my sense of gratitude, laughter is a path to walk me there. Laughter opens the window of perspective that then allows gratitude to blow into the musty corners of my being. Perhaps laughter is tied to a different quality in your life experience? What qualities does laughter draw out in you?

Talk About Everything That's gone Right In the Day

Steve Maraboli, host of Empowered Living Radio, said to me, "It's the best kind of tired when at the end of the day you've left it on the field and all your pockets are empty." This is not a negative statement, but a reference to giving your all. The way news is broadcast in this country is material for a very difficult conversation. "The news" carries such an intrinsic negative message that when we have news of the positive sort, we must qualify it by saying, "Now here's the good news."

Cultivate the habit of telling friends what has gone right, what is worth noting for its joy and lesson and verve. Join in conversations with, "Something like that happened to me once," and if it must be about a disaster, then make sure the story you tell includes something about a disaster averted, not just a disaster. Bad news is, of course, present in every life experience. It knows how to take up plenty of room on its own. I figure, why make even larger space for it by telling tales of woes? I'd rather aspire to speaking of all that has gone well.

Even in facing the most difficult circumstances with my friend D. R. when she was engaged with two different types of invasive cancer, we found the road of laughter connected us to gratitude. She is the first to acknowledge that her sense of humor and finding things to laugh about lined her path of healing and recovery. I remember vividly our jolly exchange the day her doctor suggested nuclear medicine (literally injecting her with radioactive isotopes) as a treatment for her stage-three cancer. Pondering the implications, she seriously asked her doctor, "Does this mean I won't have to use my night-light for a few weeks?" Laughter has allowed D. R. to see things that have gone well, even on some of the worst days of her illness.

My friend Mollyshannon recounted to me what elements of a public presentation of mine had really stayed with her. I appreciated hearing how she heard my words as she quoted back to me:

> You tell the tale of your life by the stories you
> repeat in your days. Does this mean my life is
> absent difficulties? Of course not. I have health
> challenges and issues with finances and friends
> who are ill. My life is filled with elements that are
> less than ideal. But that is not the story I tell. That
> is not what I spend my emotional investments on.
> The story I tell is the story of recovery, discovery,

> **You tell the tale of your life by the stories you repeat in your days.**

and uncovering. Those are the stories I repeat in my days.

The really good stories bear repeating . . . and those are the stories of laughter that lead me to my sense of gratitude.

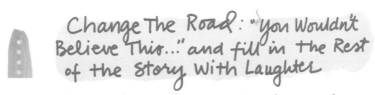

Change The Road: "You Wouldn't Believe This..." and fill in the Rest of the Story With Laughter

Joy is everywhere. It takes open eyes to see it and an open heart to appreciate it.

I promised myself to see words. I'm due to complete a project, and I was pretty sure at the start of the day that I was promising to fold myself utterly into my task. Ahhhh. I also told myself that meant no second-guessing, no turning away of ideas, and everything would be considered. And all of those ideas that wanted to be considered came knocking. Quickly. They arrived as if by a magic invitation. Dang. It's just that I thought I invited words that would be written in my book and what I got instead were words of adventure and joy lived out in the experience of my day.

Rather than turning to the dark side of expectation and disappointment, that nasty one-two punch, I opened myself to the whole winter solstice day. I gave and was gifted with words. Better than what I could have imagined. I had the heart to see the words that came courting. They indeed were everywhere. Just not dressed as I initially anticipated. They were dressed in experience and fun opportunity. And so it is with laughter. We all experience things that are only funny when we look back on them. The real joy occurs when we can laugh in the midst of the experience, as it unfolds.

In her unfolding recovery, my friend D. R. hopped on an electric-scooter shopping cart. She'd been bed-bound for over two weeks and her cabin fever got the best of her and her caregiver. They went for what seemed like a simple shopping expedition. D. R. quipped that she was already nuclear-powered by virtue of the medicine that had been pumped into her veins, and she charged off on that scooter with the same high-powered verve! Even though the end-cap display of canned green beans was the visible evidence of the tight corner she turned, and product was splayed all over the grocery store floor, D. R. could not keep from laughing. Her caregiver slipped aisles away in an effort to control her laughing fit. Even the store employee whose job it would be to recover all the cans saw the humor in the event. It has produced a new nickname, and we're talking about the source of an excellent children's story found in the expanded tales of "Scooter G. Beanes."

Relax into the natural Embrace of the Day

Live an obligation-free life; serve the debts of history and the promise of the future; bring harm to no one; live with profound meaning and positive impact; be willing to see an old thing in a new way; be willing to be financially rewarded for sincere and authentic effort. Stand ready to be utterly healthy and completely responsible to wellness; cultivate and maintain a strong immune system and a consistent energy; embrace the structures that guarantee strength and wellness and continually build upon them with information and knowledge. Express gratitude for all the influences in life. Ease into the natural embrace and flow of the day and maintain a cadence that is realistic and reflects your fundamental intentions.

A revived threat arrived in the mail, announcing intended legal action on an issue I thought was long ago put to rest. Many issues impacting my health and wellness remain unresolved. And yet I had a great day. I took appropriate action on those large, looming issues and then gave myself to the next thing in my day. I have lived another way—the way in which the yet unresolved issues cloud my joy and muddy the colors of my garden. I choose this better way. I relaxed into the natural embrace of the day. I enjoyed the many gifts that came my way. I recognize that those challenges will again call my name. And when they do, I will answer them at that time, in that day.

Winged Thoughts

I embrace my day with wide-eyed commitment.

I work independently and swim without resistance in the sea of my own creativity.

I am grateful for the grace of silence and being left to my own devices.

Judgments rail ultimately against those who speak them, not me.

We laugh to survive . . . then, with gratitude, we thrive.

It's a trade-off to maintain daily equilibrium. One worry traded for one gratitude. Shift!

May all you give circle back to you in gratitude.

Promises to Myself • • • • •

If you find yourself taking things a little too seriously, commit to seeking the opportunity for joy by bringing into your day promises to laugh.

Be grateful

Statistically, the probability of any one of us being here is so small that you'd think the mere fact of existing would keep us all in a contented dazzlement of surprise.

—Lewis Thomas

- I promise to connect with gratitude at all points in the day.
- "A thankful heart is a circular gift."
- TODAY—be dazzled by everything; let all things be a gift; participate in wonder and surprise.

Authentically Amused

There are some things so serious you have to laugh at them.

—Niels Bohr

- I promise to intensely embrace all of my passionate life and take nothing too seriously.
- "It's of such consequence that I must laugh."
- TODAY—see the irony peppered in the consequences of the world; laugh while doing all you can; consider levity the leverage in all your actions.

Practice Perspective

All know that the drop merges into the ocean,
but few know that the ocean merges into the drop.

—Kabir

- "I promise to enjoy contrasts."
- "Understand the large is found in the small."
- TODAY—it all matters, every bit. Everything is important and nothing matters. Lighten up: laugh.

We laugh to survive.

chapter 6

Forgiveness

choose with no regret

*Staying in the moment means you hardly ever have to forgive yourself—
or anyone else—or ask for forgiveness.*

—Jan Johnson

Key in Johnson's phrase are the words "hardly ever." This is not a rigid formulation. The lines between choosing with no regret and offering forgiveness to yourself—or others—can be fuzzy. I offer up that they are in partnership. Your choices stand, etched in history. Regrets aside, there is no change to be made. Forgiveness allows you to embrace your choices and accept them in the context of where you stand today.

 ## a gift of grace to myself

Set aside dogma and allow your doctrine to be defined by the way you embrace your day. Ah, would you know what I believe? Watch me live. Observe how I go to sleep at night and see me greet the morning. In my ways you will see my beliefs. My doctrine is the liturgy of my day: it is read from the pulpit of the dawn and published in the parish pews of the paths I walk and the roads I drive. It is the light that shines and is both practical and practice-able.

Celebrate Seeing the Door to Change

Many of us march through life announcing we want control, don't take well to change, and don't like surprises. This is a formula for continual struggle. The soil of struggle is the playground for change. And if you've ever seen a single flower blooming in a crack it has pushed through cement—or a wildflower blossoming in the snow—then you know life is full of surprises. A promotion. Children losing their lives before their parents. A gift delivered unexpectedly. An unkind word. Surprises are like licorice: they come in many different colors.

I celebrate seeing the door to change. Seeing the opportunity helps me be less resistant to it. Viewing myself as a perennial student informs me that I have so much to learn. I used to listen to anyone saying almost anything, nodding my head and asserting, "I know. I know." I was seeking the stamp of approval for already knowing what they were trying to tell me. I have come to recognize the value of not knowing. Of listening to words and wondering, even if they are familiar, if I can hear something new in their lyrics. I am breathless, too, at the door of change swinging open and hitting me on the nose. I keep my eyes on that door—so I can happily walk toward it and help it open.

The Road to Restorative Sleep

In the space of stillness following a long exhale—our truth speaks.
—Caren Albers

This offers an understanding of the instruction, "Take a deep breath," which must predate the metabolic grasp of the long exhalation.

That which I hold . . . releases.

That which I hide . . . reveals.

That which I inhibit . . . becomes relevant.

I exhaled into my sleep and breathed out betrayals and sorrows, assumptions and bright, shiny bitterness that I carried around in a spiritual jewelry case. Why? Deceived by their sparkle, I thought they were pretty, worthy of my attention, or precious. In the light cast by an encompassing morning, all these things are seen in the more accurate metaphor—covered with slimy, hanging moss usually reserved for the waterlogged underbelly of an old dock.

In the drying breath of the long exhale, in the truth of my own stillness, I see those insidious hitchhikers of my soul, and I no longer offer them transport. In my exhalation, they are borne away on the wind of my deep breath. My breath, which is strengthened and empowered by my desire to move beyond the willfully carried encumbrances of my past into the ecstatic ease of being present to this forgiving moment.

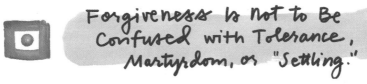

Forgiveness Is Not to Be Confused with Tolerance, Martyrdom, or "Settling."

David, my husband, has taught me a lot about responsibility for my own stuff. Until I met David, I never saw the number of fights I actually started, and how much I gave my power away with this accusation, "You make me feel like I'm a _____ (fill in the blank)." Eleanor Roosevelt said that no one could make us feel poorly about ourselves without our permission. David helped me to see what she meant by that.

Eleanor, a woman with plenty of reasons to start fights, hardly ever did. She was more interested in positive outcomes than blame or disagreements.

Though David does not satisfy my investigative penchant for understanding motivation, he does satisfy my longing to live in the present moment. If he has a motto etched on his forehead, it is "That was then, this is now."

He has zero tolerance for fight baiting or for blame. If I'm cranky, feisty, or testy and want to tangle, he'll just say, "What is it you want to accomplish here?" or, more maddeningly, he'll calmly say, "I'm not going to participate in this. I love you and I'll talk to you later." And he'll leave the room.

As in all things, that profound self-possession and control has its swing vote in bullheadedness and believing at times, when I offer up a contradicting opinion to his, that he'll do the "I know what I'm talking about" stomp-stomp dance. I have learned the appropriate response to that is, "I'm speaking from my own experience and my love for you. So having said that I'm now going to go _____ (do anything but this) and talk to you later." In all, it's been a good set of sentences for our relationship, and I've learned them from him.

I've come to see in true terms that most of the time when I start to open a can of whoop ass on someone, it's really about me. Not them. Even a tearful sense of "We don't have as many sharing moments these days as we used to" is about me. My energy level. My attitude toward my own commitments and obligations. Not allowing another person to determine our viewpoints or validate our beings or experience comes to its most significant role in our key intimate relationships.

A friend mentioned her spouse was manic about doing, achieving, preparing for his oldest friend's visit. She said his energy has been mostly in the morning since his most recent heart attack, which he "sort of" survived. After she blew off some girlfriend-to-girlfriend steam, I wondered aloud if his irrational yelling at her was really self-recrimination. Yelling in frustration for all the things he can't do or achieve and when it's so hard for him to be doing and going and getting around. He wonders at the top of his lungs how she can sit still and have fun. How dare she have fun?

So that yelling pushes all her buttons. Why? Are you less than accepting of who you are? Do you fully embrace your strengths? Does it matter if the neighbors can hear you? Does he live his life trying to be under the radar and wanting you to be quiet and unnoticed, too? If he was actually looking for a shhh-shhh quiet girl in a wife, does he fully understood he went and stood in the wrong line? We usually choose people who complete us or compel us, don't we? Although it's no fun for a friend or loved one to chew on us, in the process it is possible to wonder if it might not be all about us.

Are you bringing the full banquet to the table or are you hiding the whole who of you?

My measure and motivation are both love when I am communicating with David. I don't have twenty years of stomped feelings to contend with. But if I did, I would have to say they are my stomped feelings.

I asked my friend—Are you staying? Going? Are you bringing the full banquet to the table or are you hiding the *whole* who of you in this relationship? You can't try pen names with somebody who knows your name. He has buttons, too. Do you know how to push them? And don't you? And admit it, don't you rather enjoy the retribution?

What do you need? Maybe a domestic assistant. You're successful and of a certain age. There are people who actually choose to clean toilets for a living. They are good at it, efficient, and charge by the hour. There are structures that can be shifted to produce different results. For years I've appreciated the gentle but firm teaching of Professor Albert (yes, Einstein): "If you want different results, you must change your actions. It's insane to keep doing the same thing, over and over, and expect a different result."

Martyr. There—I've said it. It's an archetype. And, I'll confess, an ugly and lifelong tendency of mine. It's more tolerable if I call it an archetype. And the type of whipping I'm talking about here is metaphorical. Verbal. Poor treatment of some sort.

It sounds something like this. You might recognize it:

I'll take the whip. Go ahead, whip me. I stand tall.
I'll smile. I'll presume to be superior to you because
I will never whip you. No, I won't whip you . . . but
I'll make you pay in other ways. Ways that make me
look really good. Go ahead. Whip me . . . I'll take it
until I bleed. Look, I'm bleeding. Oh dear, poor me.

And maybe when he sees me bleeding, he'll say, "Sorry." Or maybe he'll just be sorry. Maybe he'll notice how tolerant and loving and patient I've been . . . just taking this whipping until I bleed.

Although it seems that the whipper never notices that the whipped is bleeding, another possibility exists. Something in him is answered by the process of (metaphorical) whipping. And something in the person being whipped is answered by the willingness to bleed.

For me, it allows me later to demonstrate what a good and tolerant person I am. "Look at what I endured for years. I bled all those years."

I work hard to notice when the Martyr wants to be my partner. It is not a successful association.

I began the shift years ago. Before I was even aware of the specter of martyrdom. I finally understood that my older brother wasn't just behaving like everyone else's older brother does. I finally grasped that he was harming me. And I hit him with a right hook that sprained my wrist. I can't remember the precise harm I brought to his bloody nose, but I know I hurt him. After that, he stopped hurting me. There's no fun in it when the desired outcomes aren't met. I no longer feared him, and I was prepared to defend myself.

In my twenties, another shift occurred. I read about ACoA: Adult Children of Alcoholics. I thought I was so unique in my challenges and pain, and then I looked around and understood there were millions of "us." Souls raised in the shadow of alcoholism but without the alcohol in our own veins to dull the pain. So unhealthy structures to dull, protect, and hide became the medication, instead of drugs or alcohol.

These behavioral addictions are challenging to kick because on the outside they make me look like:

A) the nice one;

B) the good girl;

C) the giver;

D) the negotiator.

In truer terms they should be called:

A) doormat;

B) martyr;

C) dupe—pouring an endless pitcher;

D) compromiser.

Certainly, these are less endearing titles but sometimes more accurate.

Well. Books have been written on this subject and subjects that evolve out of it. As for me, I won't be writing a book on it any time soon. I find it as elusive as a beautiful butterfly: almost winging to a landing on my outstretched hand . . . and then, floating away on the wind. Sometimes I get it. Sometimes I don't.

But what I do know is this. I've had the separate bedroom and the divorce that followed. I have been through some of the challenges that Eleanor Roosevelt faced. And Eleanor is right. No one can make me feel poorly about myself without my permission.

How about you?

Who's in charge of how you feel about yourself?

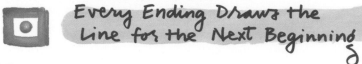

Every Ending Draws the Line for the Next Beginning

The trees. The trees do so many important things—without effort their tree-ness is adequate. They stand tall. Provide home to many other life-forms. Oxygenate. Hold fast the ground. Absorb lightning and allow time and natural elements to heal wounds to their being. As they bend in the wind, there's no tree saying, "I must be more flexible." They are just as flexible as they are—no more, no less. As they bend in the wind, there's no tree saying, "I must be more proactive." They allow endings and beginnings, the natural cycle, and do what they do best: be a tree.

> *He that cannot forgive others*
> *breaks the bridge over which he himself must pass.*
> —George Herbert

Forgiveness. When the circumstances requiring forgiveness from others involve continual, consistent bad behavior, it creates a conundrum. It is a challenging balance between letting go with forgiveness and finding a way not to engage with the unacceptable behavior.

Forgiveness is not to be confused with tolerance or accommodation. One friend of mine feared forgiveness. He thought it meant saying, "I forgive you for breaking my nose," and then standing there so his nose could be broken again.

Forgiveness for behaviors doesn't imply continued allowance of the behavior. Forgiveness dissolves the resentment, releases the anger, and resolves potential bitterness. Forgiveness allows the clarity of acceptance of circumstance to seep in, or sometimes it rushes in. This underscores that forgiveness is always self-serving. It is an invitation to personal freedom from the shackles that tie to unfavorable conditions or actions.

Dealing with continual poor practices is one thing. Forgiveness is quite another. Rather than the offended person becoming inured to the offense, forgiveness lets fresh air into the murky, musty room of muddled thinking and breathes renewed lucidity into the challenging circumstance(s).

Choosing with no regret and forgiveness are inextricably tied. It does not mean I can declare that all the choices in my life have been good ones. Hardly. I can say that I love where I stand today. In that, I have no regret for the choices I have made. Those choices have all conspired to bring me to this moment. At that intersection of loving my present and forgiving my past is a place of balance and peace.

 Winged Thoughts

Roll out the red carpet on the kind of day that you want.

The most undesirable events are immediately soothed by forgiveness and love.

My past brought me here, but I am not my past.

I arrived here as a survivor, and I move on as a thriver.

I hold on to my sorrows. Why? I must have thought they were pretty.

I identify myself as a continuous, strong thriver.

Forgiveness is not to be confused with tolerance or accommodation.

Word Birds

Word Birds

The opposite of a closed mind is willingness, and an awakened heart does not embrace everything . . . it is awake to everything and willfully chooses with what it will encircle.

Restoration is a return to what was; transformation is a transition to what shall be and is often marked by forgiveness.

Walking in cadence with your choices makes every journey a journey of joy.

Let the weights of your past be not a weight to hold you but rather a stabilizing factor from which you draw continuous lessons.

Your obligations (will be and), in truth, are met . . . time just needs to catch up.

Being alive is a fierce responsibility. What will you do with everything that is possible today?

Demonstrate an extraordinary talent for making the world a healthier place, one choice at a time.

We tell the tale of our lives by the choices we repeat in our days.

Promises to Myself • • • • •

Can you begin to partner with forgiveness and make choices without regret? If there is a more appropriate combination for you, then make it and set a few promises for yourself.

Highest good

To transform the world we must begin with ourselves.
—J. Krishnamurti

• I promise to act in my own best interest.

• "Choose your own highest good in all ways."

• TODAY—compassion toward yourself is the first measure; breathe!; service to others is built upon service to self; acknowledge that self-care is investment in the highest good.

Small graces

Of many small graces are grand endeavors built.
—mar

• I promise to honor each small grace as part of my large vision.

• "Every choice matters—no matter how insignificant it appears."

• TODAY—experience the satisfaction that is available in all your tasks; each thing is valuable regardless of size; see the extraordinary in the ordinary.

Clarity's Magic

It is not meaning we need but sight.
—Lawrence Durrell

• I promise to allow lucidity to enliven the corners of my day.

• "Clearness can transform all your choices."

• TODAY—set aside the extraneous for the essential; follow the path of the pertinent; permit translucence to travel from within and without. Be transparent.

Create Legacy

A line is a dot that went for a walk.
—Paul Klee

• I promise to do things that matter.

• "Invest yourself wholly in matters of consequence; do not become absorbed by the trivial."

• TODAY—let go of the small actions; write; study. Dispense efficiently with the perfunctory and move to the planned and purposeful: allow for alchemy.

breath
breathe

chapter 7

Enthusiasm

continue to learn

"Dream it. Do it. Be it." My friend Barbara Mundell shared that this is one of the many mottos for her life. And closer investigation into the way she unfolds her days demonstrates she stays true to this motto, as well as to so many others. Barb recounts her views on centuries of mystery and wisdom with rare understanding and much enthusiasm. It's never surprised me that ravens and crows are favored birds and bird images of hers. She is drawn to learning the way a raven is pulled toward a small sparkling object. Her way of expressing an intentional life is, "Living your imperative."

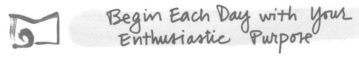 ### Begin Each Day with Your Enthusiastic Purpose

Being connected to your enthusiasm is a great deal of fun, brings vibrancy and zest to each part of the day, and throws doors in your experience wide open.

There are some requirements. You must (be willing to) set aside ego and any attachment you have to looking smart or sophisticated. The interests must lie in discovery and presence, not appearance and assessment. The instant the familiar question "What will people think?" is asked, enthusiasm evaporates. Enthusiasm prefers the company of freedom and unself-consciousness.

A service provider and I speak often about her childhood dream of being a dancer. Her dream was deferred in adulthood and traded for more practical pursuits. Regularly, we make the case for dance finding a place in her every day.

She returned the compliment recently, observing my "dancing hands" and remembering to me the pleasure of movement with a ribbon tied with a swivel to the end of a stick.

> If you are a student, there are teachers everywhere.

"Oh, yes!" I recalled all the ways that the ribbons can be moved. It is like writing with color in the air. I made a note to self: find one. And I did. Wandering through a toy store I came upon them unexpectedly (seizing serendipity is another favorite thing of enthusiasm), I noticed the ribbon sticks. One for each hand came home with me. Parked on the ferry dock, I unwrapped one ribbon while standing alongside my car. When I am professionally engaged with children, we do an exercise called air write. It's like finger painting only without the paint and paper—we write in the air. Adding a ribbon turns it into skywriting. And right there on the ferry dock I began. Oblivious. It took a man walking by, kindly laughing and observing, "You are having entirely too much fun," for me to stir to the stares and smiles from the people in the dozens of cars around me. Both were returned with a shrug and a smile. With no embarrassment, I resumed my discovery process of all the ways that ribbon would have me move it.

If you feel the need for assistance or tutoring in this celebration of your enthusiasm, there are two readily available resources. Hang out with some local three- or four-year-olds, or a big ol' dog in moist fresh-mown grass. In those classrooms, you will learn most everything you need to know to begin celebrating your native enthusiasm.

Learn as If Your Life Depended On It — It May

The adults with the best study skills are the most successful because they learn from all their life experiences, show up and listen even if it's not an enjoyable instructor. Take notes, ask questions (especially if you are not clear), study, review, test—next!

If you are a student, there are teachers everywhere.

If you are a student now, you will be committed to being a student for the remainder of your life. This is the wisest position to fill and the most important role to accept. As a student, you are positioned to learn from everything—the splinter, the hot stove, the rapid descent, the unkind word, the shunning by a group not your own, the preciousness of life and how quickly it lets go.

As a student, when you look at a flower, you see it was once a seed and that it will likely plant itself again; you see the earth; you see the bird that sow seeds afar and the insects that work both for and against that single flower.

To a student, a flower is so much more than simply a flower. It is first a stand for beauty. It is a world containing so many elements, roles, and occupations—just like you.

If you are a student, such is the richness of your sight.
An investment in knowledge pays the best interest.
—Benjamin Franklin

I used Franklin's quote as a thoughtful impetus on a particular day. *Investment* is the word that played out throughout the day, and I consistently asked myself this question: "What is this activity an investment in?" I applied that question to virtually every action.

Since I had a heightened awareness of adding knowledge to my core, I evaluated the library books I had on hand. I measured my available time and decided research reading for my next book would not pay as many immediate dividends as reading on my current health issues. A trip to the library to return those books was added to the menu of the day—and a book on the relationship of food to healing was placed on interlibrary order. Three other books came home with me, and I invested an hour in reading *Feed Your Tiger*, a book relating principles of Chinese energy medicine to eating patterns. It produced immediate behavioral changes and quite a few "aha"-accompanied discoveries.

Thanks, Benjamin, you old scoundrel. Focusing on one of his wise sayings and bringing my contemplation of it into the activities of my day produced some positive results.

What If We Just Acted Like Everything Was Easy?

Blessed are those who dream dreams
and are willing to pay the price to make them come true.
—Henry Viscardi Jr.

"Pay the price" is bootstrap-pulling-up thinking. If it's good and worthy, it must also come with a cost. I add that a dream is true in its simple act of being dreamt. A dream comes to trueness the instant I am willing for it to be true. Simple. Not complex. "What if I just pretended like everything was easy?"

Then it would be.

Dreams and their price tags . . . belong in the darkness. Dreams being real and simply and unfoldingly true belong in the lightness of our ease.

Smart and technologically literate are two different things. I contributed to the effort to persuade my chiropractor to get an iPhone. And now he views me as his resident phone specialist. I had to train for an hour with an Apple store trainer before I even got my phone. He called recently so frustrated. "I have tried everything," and then he provided a long list of all those attempts, "and I can't get my volume up so I can hear my phone ring. Help!"

I headed to his office where he promptly put the iPhone in my hand. I reflected just for a moment on this peculiar turn of events. I, who just last summer pledged to stop declaring that I was technically challenged and who marched over the water on a ferry once a week for months in order to be trained in the fundamentals of keyboard functions, was seen as a competent source of assistance for someone else's computer challenge. It was an amazing turn of events.

So, phone in hand, I asked myself, "What was the first question my favorite computer geek always asked me?"

The answer was immediate because it was always the same first question. "Is it plugged in?"

Therefore I looked, wondering, is the ringer turned on? No, it wasn't. I turned the phone faceup in the doc's hands and, without judgment and with complete empathy, I said, "This first little button here is often accidentally toggled. When you turn the sound on— see?—it gives you both the visual indicator and—feel that?—it's set to vibrate as well. Same when you turn it off."

He accepted the simplicity of the solution as his own critical judge. He groaned. "How could I have not known?" He chastised himself out loud.

I knew perfectly well the answer to his "How?" New skill sets don't immediately allow for those short intuitive paths between information yards. And we also tend to believe solutions are complex. Frequently, they are simple. I still often jump into a solution matrix that is complicated and confounding. And I have to work my way back to simplicity.

My computer language is growing daily. Abilities are building. One of the most important things is to support my learning with perspective. I stopped saying, "I'm technologically challenged," and replaced it with, "I am committed to increasing my computer skills." What a difference one sentence has made in my experience.

You are so smart. Try saying that to yourself for a few days. And then ask yourself, "What if I just pretended everything was easy?"

I set aside the drama from the trauma. Difficult conversations have their own basic challenge, and adding the festoonery of drama just dresses challenge in colorful mockery.

If I see these many challenges as bull's-eyes in a game of darts, I can approach each one with equal verve. If it were "easy," I would just play, dispatch the dart after some aim. I would not agonize over it and turn it over and over in my hand and speculate on potential outcomes. I would just throw the dart.

It would be just that easy with the events of my life—walking in a cadence that is consistent, manageable, and even playful. There is really no pretending here—it can be just that easy. And on the days that it isn't, I pretend!

Every Road's an Adventure When You Travel with Enthusiasm

Every road. Even for a metaphorical thinker, this specific day this was literally true. I drove into San Francisco on a summer Saturday. Park Presidio Boulevard was filled with people. Most people had guide-books and questioning, puzzled looks. I enjoyed vicarious discovery while proceeding precisely where my GPS directed me. To my friend's house. I traveled streets and a road quintessentially San Francisco.

A vertical climb virtually observing the oncoming view—the view was just all hill. I was reminded of the correct way to position my tires on such a steep grade, and before I knew it, I was off on another adventure with my friend. Turns out a "shortcut" through Golden Gate Park was no shortcut at all. The streets were closed for an event, but the detours created an adventure, which I enjoyed very much. I embraced the new and unanticipated views with enthusiasm.

 Winged Thoughts

Relentless creativity is my path to knowledge and discovery.

Be wowed by the speed of enthusiasm.

A dog never needs a justification to experience ecstasy at any moment.

Enthusiasm turns an ordinary activity into a memorable event.

Stepping aside from habit and certainty makes room for the fresh winds of enthusiasm and wonder.

Everything's better on the second "grow" around.

Flexibility means to go where the learning is going.

Fireworks amazement is in the combustibility of innovation.

The joys comfort me and the difficulties caution me as I allow myself to learn. I've turned my tears into teaching today.

Promises to Myself • • • • •

Approaching issues with enthusiasm requires self-confidence. Advance the role of enthusiasm in your life by including it in a promise to yourself.

Question Enthusiastically

It is better to know some of the questions than all of the answers.
—James Thurber

• I promise to ask fresh questions all day long.

• "Learn essential things by making irreverent inquiry."

• Looking into this day, this might mean—with eyes of wonder, seeing old things in new ways; being relentlessly curious; staring long in the mirror.

Create Fearlessly

[W]hat is real is not the exterior but the idea, the essence of things.
—Constantin Brancusi

• I promise to follow an enthusiastic impulse to innovation.

• "Pursue the natural progression toward unknown form."

• Looking into this day, this might mean—experimenting with unfamiliar materials, taking an unknown road, making something utterly unlike your patterns.

Practice Practice

Practice is nine-tenths.

—Ralph Waldo Emerson

- Draw upon all of life, the whole practice, to create authentically and enthusiastically.

- "Be connected to the truth of your own practice."

- TODAY—practice practice; utilize your own skill set to expand into unknown things; represent all aspects, not just what appears or feels "successful"; listen hard; appreciate what you don't know . . . honor knowing that you don't know.

Seize Synchronicity

There is nothing that can help you understand your own beliefs better than trying to explain them to an inquisitive child.

—Frank Clark

- I promise to be observant of those "little things."

- "There are divine indicators everywhere—notice."

- TODAY—take note beyond coincidence; clap your hands and say, "I believe," and maybe Tinker Bell will revive; dare to participate in the unbelievable.

chapter 8

Relationship

appreciate your friends

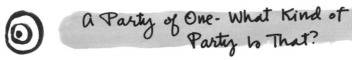

A Party of One - What Kind of Party Is That?

I consider my solitude as I sit outside. Puget Sound is at a minus tide, revealing so plainly why the expanse in front of me is called "Useless Bay." People stroll to the tide's edge at low tide, and there's no hope for a boat moored close to shore in this bay. Hence, the Useless part of the name. The whirring throaty buzz of hummingbirds comes from the feeder to my left. The songbirds are rehearsing their liturgy. The sound of fast-moving sandpaper blocks striking each other, squeaky and intermittent, comes from the crows in the trees over there. There are eagles so close I can appreciate the majesty of their white hoods from here, even without my helpful eyeglasses.

I sit soaking in this rare demonstration of Pacific Northwest spring sun. My better judgment reminds me I have more artwork to complete. Oh, yeah. This is just a pause in the day. It is a contribution to my vitamin D3 intake and an investment in my relationship to myself. The crow crowd (we don't call them a murder here) wonder if my presence means food will soon be thrown to them. They cannot imagine any other reason I would be outside. Simply sitting on the deck. We do exist only to feed them, don't we?

I remember saying to my dear friend Barb earlier today that rest and friends are two of the most important things in our lives . . . and yet in our busy-ness we often place both elements last in our day. If we manage to place them in our day at all. Aware that I have just invested in that first part of the equation—rest—I pick up my phone and call several of my cherished souls whose voices I haven't heard in a bit. Laughter and stories punctuate the birdsong. There was the second part: friends. This equation and the balance between the two are what it is to be content in a party of one. And this ease in my own company, my own "party of one" creates a way for contentment to be present in my larger circle of relationship.

Inevitably, I will dine alone when I travel. Over the years I've come to appreciate the unique opportunity that taking a meal by myself offers me. A dependable part of this experience is how restaurant staff relate to a single diner. "Just one?" they often inquire, or "A party of—one?" I've come to the habit of laughingly giving this reply: "Yes, a party of one and *what* a party it is!"

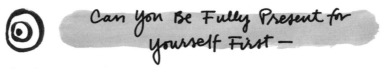

Can you Be Fully Present for Yourself First —

Like the children's literature creature going from one animal to another asking, "Are you my mother?", I have been searching for a sense of home all my life. In relationships outside my blood family, in places, in shiny shells set up with colorful walls and complementary furniture. In spite of the fact that I have written, "When I say I am going home, I mean I am going where you are," the hard and contradictory truth is, "I am my own home."

Home is an answer of place from deep within me. Recently, in the face of a loving but frustrated litany of "Here's what's not quite right about you," I've recognized that someone else's assessment of me is not a depressing truth. It's just their truth. In spite of being paired in marriage and added in to the lives of many cherished friends, I really am one, alone at the end of any of these relational equations. I have an incredibly supportive circle. Increasingly, while I honor the spiritual value of friendship and intimate relationship, I must acknowledge I enter my dreams alone, I walk the halls of my nightmare fears alone, and I press forward into growth and understanding, acceptance and personhood alone. "A party of one." Yes, indeed and what a party it is. Being attentive to that single party first and before others is what enables me to be in dynamic relationship with others. I take care of myself, first. Then I am confident I am able to give, from wholeness and fullness, to my larger circle.

 Being attentive Has So many Rewards

The call to serve takes many forms in the life of a compassionate heart.

—mar

Listen better and be more respectful toward yourself and you will be more respectful and celebratory of the stories your friends tell. They are telling them for a reason. Especially if it's the seventh time they are telling it! If a friend says something shocking like wanting to "punch someone," withhold your judgment. Instead of correcting them or offering your alternative action, try inquiry, "Why?" Or observation, "Oh, you feel like punching them, eh?" Just as some pharmaceuticals act as a potentiate for other drugs, so do we serve that function in our friendships. A friend takes what is already working and helps raise it up a notch or two. In this model, being attentive to your relationship to yourself allows the same sort of capacity to dial up what is working within you. I remind myself of this truth as often as I remind my circle of friends: tending to our own needs, first, is the finest way to be in service to each other.

When I was almost six, I grasped that Mother's Day meant doing something really special and significant for your mother. How very much I wanted to be grown up and do the right thing on a holiday. I gathered the pennies that my family provided me when I did something of value around the house. I think I had a double fistful, which must have been just shy of fifty cents. It felt like a treasure chest full of money to me!

Happily, I slipped out of the house and, like a very big girl, walked the two and a half blocks to Tooze Florist on Stark Street. I reached up, piled my riches on the counter, and proudly announced, "I'm here to get something wonderful for my mother for Mother's Day." Only decades later did I come to understand the pressures mounted on a flower business the Friday before Mother's Day. The most demanding day in a florist's entire year!

It was a balding man who smiled and scooped up my pile of money. He asked me exactly what did I want? I surveyed the large store. Corsages! My sister, Judy, had given ladies at her wedding corsages. That must be a really cool thing. If it was good for a once-in-a-lifetime wedding, it'd be good for a mother's holiday. Proud of my decision, I announced, "A corsage."

He gave me the choice of having it delivered or waiting while he made it. The immediate satisfaction of gift giving has been with me a very long time. "Now!" I said, reasoning why wait until Sunday when she could have it now—all the more days to enjoy it. That dear man stopped what he was doing and made a glorious, very large corsage. He placed it in a big waxed bag. It rested on the end of a large fern. He folded over the edge and put a large pin through the end of the bag. Wow. I watched his every move with fascination. It was the most beautiful thing I'd been involved with in my young life. After he placed the corsage in my hand, he gave me a dime. He told me I'd overpaid him. Of course, I believed him since I'd hauled two fistfuls of coin in there. I had no idea of the enormity of the compassionate generosity I'd just received.

As can happen, my profoundly earnest effort was not met with the anticipated joy. After I festively, dancingly presented my Happy Mother's Day present, I was heatedly questioned and was promptly walloped. My mother was horrified. She understood the cost of what she held in her hand, and she was convinced I had to have stolen it from the local flower shop. Reasoning that I was not inclined toward theft carried no impact.

"I bought it with my own money. Really." I even produced the dime change to prove that I had more than enough to purchase this honor for her on Mother's Day.

Her horror gave way to embarrassment. She filled in the generous corners of the story.

A grabbed coat. The hat donned. The purse retrieved from its spot. My mother snagged my hand, and I was dragged at a rapid clip to the flower shop. I greeted the bald man like the old and dear friend he had become. My mother greeted him by name.

> As can happen, my profoundly earnest effort was not met with the anticipated joy.

"Wow, she knows everybody," I thought.

They spoke in whispered tones. It escalated into what I recognized as a restrained argument. There was a lot of head shaking and no saying on both their parts. I saw that my mother finally made some other kind of purchase because she pulled money out of her wallet. I guessed that she had chosen to wait for the "delivery" option because, unlike me, she walked out of the shop with nothing of beauty in her hand. Just my hand, firmly grasped. The walk back home wasn't as fast.

She was softer on the way home. After she hung up her coat and put away her hat, she had a little talk with me. The particulars elude me now. I suspect they eluded me then, too. I can only guess that it was about the true value of money and learning my lesson. I do remember the word "embarrassment" figured in somewhere. And I remember that she did thank me for my gift.

My own experience as a young girl with money and the miracles that come from the compassionate kindness of strangers shape my attitude toward family and gifting. The joy, for me, isn't so much in the response of the receiver. It's in that first impulse of longing to create a gift for another. That's the real value of a gift. It is from that place that the gift gets given back in so many unexpected ways. That "giveback" is like the dime I held in the palm of my hand as a sincere five-year-old.

The other thing I know now that I didn't know then is that my mother *did* carry a thing of beauty in her hand back home. Me. Whether she saw it or not, my action was based in true intent and honest affection. There's beauty in that, even when it's not recognized.

We listen. We listen. We move. We sit. It rains. The sun comes out. There stands a friend. We listen. We laugh. We share. We sit. We move. It rains. There stands a friend. We listen. We share. We sit. We move. The sun comes up. There. I stand a friend.

No Day Is Wasted in Which a Single Moment Is Spent on Love

No lacy red hearts. Just encouragement, support, and living to the edge of my self. Truth telling is love and holding your tongue, listening hard, accepting responsibility, remaining quiet, and holding on to a new story in order to hear, for the second time, someone else's story.

Looking and holding a glance. Touching an elbow while wordlessly walking past, willingly and joyfully accepting coffee in bed. Cooking dinner as well as clearing the dishes. Love is both uncompromising and making compromise. Love dresses as the grandest of contradictions and wears colorful garments made with asymmetrical balance.

If You Have One Friend, You Hold the Hand of the World

Friendship is the only cement that will ever hold the world together.
—Woodrow Wilson

A scene from *Tombstone* with Val Kilmer portraying Doc Holliday remains vivid in my memory. Doc's hauled himself off his deathbed to help a group of men defend his friend Wyatt Earp. The defenders were shocked to see him. They thought he should be in bed, and they questioned him:

"Whadya doin' here?"

"Wyatt's my friend."

One of the guys said, "Hey, I got a lot of friends."

After a pause, Doc said, simply, "I don't."

We are all connected. Two friends contacted me today asking for prayerful support. And two other friends called me today telling me they were praying for my health. Those were "old" friends, people woven long into my history. A friend called me to explore a possibility of mutual benefit. We discussed the opportunity and ultimately decided no was the best answer.

All day long, my friends filled in, like mortar between the building bricks of my events and experiences. One greets another through me. Our shared connections bond us exponentially. Yes, in a large view, relationships/friendships do hold the world together. In the micro, my up-close worldview, my friends, in many instances, hold me together.

We hold you close, with open hands, to help you stand strong.
We hold you close, with hands clasped in prayer, that you will stand tall.
Whether you are near or far . . . you are ever embraced in our hearts and prayers.

Remembering our naming and embracing
A new name by remembering the old one . . .

To remember . . . embrace your
Love and hold her hand and
Whisper how precious
How precious is your breath.

To remember . . .
Honor your friend and set aside the
Indulgence of regret. Extend your
Hand now and rest your arm on
The strength of your choices.

To remember . . .
Rise a little earlier and wrap your
Intuition around the world.

To remember . . .
Gift a stranger, support an aching heart
With anonymous care, walk more
Gently and thank the roots of your favorite
Tree for all their work.

To remember . . .
Shout the anger of loss down the canyons
Of mystery and open your arms,
Ready, for the next birth in which
They will assist.

Light a candle . . .
Bridge the miles of stupefying loss
And know that only little graces,
Little stones, rebuild the wall
Which is hope.

     And this wall becomes,
     Again, the shelter for
     Many unspoken sobs: here
     There is safety and
     Protected healing.

Light a candle to remember and
Then sleep. Deeply sleep. When you
Awaken the world awaits your
Next loving song. Because of the
Strength of your remembering and
The profound love with which
You hold your friend—you will sing.

Winged Thoughts

Another person may not determine my viewpoint or validate my being or experiences. It is an asset when I know where the "me" ends and the "us" begins.

We choose people who complete us or compel us.

Remember your promises to each other . . . may your love prompt new promises, and may your love renew your vows on the difficult days. May your laughter answer many questions, and may you reach the finest places in your heart with each other.

Go ahead, weep for the rare, the never-seen-just-this-way-again, unmitigated beauty of love.

Love is visibly measured with action.

We honor numbers and recognize days . . . the memories we create with friends are what we treasure forever.

Appreciate the open hand of your friend.

Truth telling is the strongest bonding agent.

Yes, so much to do and miles to go, and nowhere more important to stand than by the side of your friend.

Friendship sings solidly but quietly from the corners of our days.

It's rewarding communication when we tell others what it is we are hoping for rather than waiting for them to guess.

 Winged Thoughts

Word Bird

Recognize your many choices, and encourage yourself with these two words: "Choose love."

Difficult truths serve better when spoken during the day rather than collected toward one magnificent explosion.

Grow a new kind of family tree: one chosen from joy, not obligation. Just as in the natural world . . . this tree will change with the seasons of your life.

Quantity is more helpful as a measurement in recipes than in friendships.

As the utmost of all priority, friends trump almost everything.

Our love, a door. We pass in patience and compassion and always walk the path of love and commitment home.

We build together—ever outward in patience and compassion; ever inward with respect and adoration. Our love, fearless and unrelenting, fuels our respect and patience for each other and our capacity for compassionate service for the world.

Promises to Myself •••••

Do you want to incorporate a deeper awareness of relationship into your day? Craft some promises to yourself that can integrate your commitment to yourself with your commitment to friends and family.

Honor Friendship

When you have one friend, you hold the hand of the world.
—mar

- I promise to appreciate my faraway friends.
- "Demonstrate that each friend is a gift to you by using your skill set."
- TODAY—make something and mail it; write something and post it; name your friends and pray for their highest good, speak their names and tell stories about them.

Embrace Interconnectedness

Each friend represents a world in us, a world possibly not born until they arrive and it is only by this meeting that a new world is born.
—Anaïs Nin

- I promise to extend myself to strangers.
- "Have the openness to allow a stranger to become a friend."

• Looking into this day, this might mean—engaging in an unexpected exchange, reaching out to a "friend of a friend," broadening your circle.

Courageously Unconventional

Curious things, habits. People themselves never knew they had them.
—Agatha Christie

• I promise to behave/think outside habitual structures.

• "You are unlimited in your ability to be inventive."

• Looking into my day, this might mean—writing/working in bed instead of at my desk, asking for help when I'd do it myself, delivering different messages to friends, surprising my friends (and myself) at tonight's event.

Love is visibly measured with action.

chapter 9

Dream

do what you love

 May your Heart Be awakened to all your Dreams

Willingness. Just be willing to see, observe, consider. The opposite of a closed mind is willingness. An awakened heart does not mean the heart embraces everything; it means that it is awake to everything and willfully chooses with what and which it will encircle. Being awakened to my dreams simply expands my sense of options and possibility at every juncture.

 Show your Dreams to the World

It takes a lot of courage to show your dreams to someone else.
—Erma Bombeck

I've been showing my dreams to the world in my writing for a good portion of my life. I share my dreams in my social networks. I write them on whiteboard and on my walls. It strikes me that people think courage is required to speak your dreams because someone might belittle them or minimize the dream when it is shown.

I can be grateful for early childhood education in how to manage dream minimization. I learned early how to respond to "You can't do that." Why argue? Just do it.

Mostly, when it comes to dreams, I emphasize that I don't care what others think. I can join Rumi in climbing up and "From the rooftops, shout your joy." In my lifetime folks have often thought of me as shamelessly self-promoting. They have not understood that I am celebrating my surprise and delight that one of my dreams has worked its way up to the roof and is busy shouting, "I came true. Somebody dreamed me into reality. Look!"

do what you love

It happens periodically. The transcendent moment when craft transports a creative to a holy place, a place of sacred athleticism. Where silence and sound meet, where engaging with art becomes a physical exertion. It is an exercise in inspiration. It is exhilarating and exhausting.

I remember gymnastics and the feeling of dismounting the horse. I knew when every motion had been in perfect succession and I had "nailed it." So it is with one's craft. Any craft. My experience is with the craft of writing. Some rare days I get it right the first time, perfection as I leave the pommel horse of my work.

A writer writes. Every day. It is the work, the practice of the craft. Edit. Sculpt phrases. Cross out words. Replace words or eliminate them. Hold sentences to the light, turn them, confirm balance. When the words sparkle, put them back and move on. That is the work, consistently. Hemingway acknowledged the everydayness of good writing by confessing that, generally, out of thousands of words in a day, a writer is bound to seize upon fifty good ones. And so it goes, most of the time.

Those "everyday" days pave the road on the journey for the luminous moment. That moment when experience agrees with immediacy and they inform the spirit of any permission ever granted toward grace. And they work in synergistic, committed cadence to produce something extraordinary. That is the incandescent crossroad on the journey. The markers and signs read anew as the road of creating moves on. The trick is to embrace the ordinary, lovingly, each day, on its own dependable merit. Each mile on the road is indeed drawing closer to another brilliant intersection (as the ordinary invites the extraordinary). There is more road than crossroad and one cannot be held in value over the other. They are inseparable.

Lucidity has varying measures of shine and each day spent pursuing the passion of craft is brilliant in its own way.

What Art Does— The Kennedy Center Honors

Writer, composer, actor, director, and producer Mel Brooks; pianist and composer Dave Brubeck; opera singer Grace Bumbry; actor, director, and producer Robert De Niro; and singer and songwriter Bruce Springsteen.

I like to watch one awards show each year. This is the one. The one that acknowledges with full national force the significant role that the arts play in the life of America. The work of my day was put away. I turned off my phone. For two hours I was transported. Commercial breaks were taken in conversation with my husband about what we had just seen. Each performer honored had a place of significance in our histories.

And tonight their stories were part of my story. Because that is what art does. It engages. It draws you in. It's the train wreck you have to watch, and it's the prolonged note, the beauty of which pulls across the skin of your life like a knife and draws blood. ART. It's not the neat and the orderly. It is the inspiring and the impacting. It's immediate. Dangerous. And essential.

As Bruce Springsteen's music ran its full brush across the palette of the evening, I saw it again. The art of America stirring the soul. I saw the memories playing on the screens of every person in attendance there in the Kennedy Center. In my home and homes within the broadcast reach. Springsteen's lyrical presence, like Whitman, like Sandburg, uniquely calls out that which is undeniably American in our experience. They were dancing. They were clapping. They could not remain still. They, we, were calling to mind that which once was. That's what art does. It calls to mind that which was before and brings it again, alive, in this moment. Not predictable and anticipated but wild and utterly breath-stealing.

My husband and I dried our tears. I uttered a holy expletive under my breath and declined bed for a bit. "I have to write."

I am compelled. Because *that* is what art does.

Leverage the opportunities that work for you: pave the way and seize the clear opportunity regardless of where you are.

When I am aligned with passion and right action, questions of self-knowing fall away. "Who am I?" and "What is my dream?" are answered in the authentic impulses that punctuate my days.

Clarity visits and leaves no footprints, only dreams.

It is a precious homecoming to return to my dreams after being long away from them.

 you go where your Thoughts go

A man's life is what his thoughts make of it.
—Marcus Aurelius

Did my father consciously base his driving lessons on the principles of Marcus Aurelius?

My first driving lesson occurred down the road. A farmer was laying in his rows for field planting. My dad had me stand and watch the tractor drive from one end of the field to the other.

"I thought you said I was getting a driving lesson?"

"You are."

"I'm going to learn how to drive on a tractor?"

"Just watch."

At each end of the farmer's field were flimsy row markers. As he finished a row, he ran each marker over with his tractor. All this was unfamiliar to me and I equated the markers to signs, signs that had some ongoing purpose, and I commented to my dad how weird it was that he was running over the things that he had, apparently, so purposely set.

> Art calls to mind that which was before and brings it again, alive, in this moment.

"He doesn't need them anymore."

"Why?"

"Just watch. You'll figure it out."

After a while I stopped looking at the tractor and observed the farmer instead. After several more rows, I saw what my dad wanted me to see. The driver never took his eyes off the row markers. He didn't look at us, his house, or anything else. He left behind him straight, perfectly measured rows. When we walked out of the field and all the way back to the house, we talked about how driving a car was just like that. When you drive looking immediately in front of you, the vehicle is constantly adjusting, the ride isn't smooth, and turns are abrupt. When you drive with your eyes ahead, the path is smooth, the turns are anticipated, and it's a better and safer ride.

He showed me the difference between the two ways of looking. Switchback curves and hairpin turns comprise Highway 53. When he focused on the road in front of him, I almost got carsick. It was a rocky, shifting ride. When his gaze fell forward along the road, he drove to the "row marker," and the car motored smoothly.

This became a perfect metaphor for me. You naturally move toward what you're looking at, or, more to the point, you go where your thoughts go. When first standing in that field, I was certain it was the most unsuitable place in the world to learn how to drive.

What do you know? Marcus Aurelius and my dad had a few things in common.

 ## Lean Forward Into your Life

I wonder how many dawns I just poured into the paint palette? Could I explain that to someone? Many people I know who paint don't experience this extraordinary wrestling forth of the work. I know many people think of painting as "craft" or, more to the point, "production work." That is not how it is for me.

Painting is to me what the sports writer Walter Wellesy "Red" Smith said writing was for him—all he had to do was open a vein and hold his wrist over the paper. Paint is like that for me. It pours out of my veins.

The colors mix on paper right out of my soul. These forms I just painted had my longings and inspiration and breath poured into each stroke. So that when somebody looked at what I'd created, they would feel uplifted, encouraged. Supported.

And in that, the art gives back. Like a practiced faith. There's an ethereal reward, but in the immediate there is a liturgy of my creation. The ritual I must go through to paint is not conventionally recognizable. Not incense, but the vapors of my anxiety and anticipation rising. Not prayers, just formless utterings framing the unnamed sounds of my desire to communicate peace, passion, hope. And order.

There has to be order before I can make chaos. Ironically, it's taken me three days to "ready" the studio. Less than one day to mess it up with paint and splatters and painterly towels. Brushes everywhere drying.

What an appetite it makes. Thankfully, my husband, David, often calls me to dinner.

The jump is so frightening between where I am and where I want to be.
Because of all I may become I will close my eyes and leap.

—mar

When I was a little girl, I would save my money and go to our corner drugstore, which had, what I thought, was the world's largest collection of greeting cards. And they were for sale! Bliss.

I loved all the images and would take an hour to select one card. Even at eight years old, I thought the inside greetings were just plain silly. I would purchase my card, march home, and use my dad's white-strike-out-correcting sheet to set those insides right (had Wite-Out not yet been invented?). Then it was ready for a personal note and was sent off to some interested family friend or a relative who required a thank-you. I was not sure what "precocious" meant, but folks always said it in a kind way when they told my mother that's what I was.

In my early twenties, I dreamt of starting my own greeting card company. I would write on the pages of my journal, "I want to be an artist." I longed to create a livelihood that had meaning and use my talents and skills in the service of a compelling and inspiring idea. I was certain that I would have to wait until I was (eh-hem) really old. Maybe some time in my forties. I thought perhaps by the time I reached the wise age of forty-five, I would have gotten all the education needed and managed to save up enough money to fund my own company.

The rumblings wouldn't leave. I felt unwilling to wait almost twenty years before I could manifest my dream. I wrote to a man who used to own a kite shop in the small community where I lived. He knew a lot about how to make things fly . . . including one's dreams. I poured my heart out to him in that letter. I told him I realized I didn't know the first thing about operating a business, and I didn't have a dime to my name. But I knew what I wanted to do. And then I wrote, "The jump is so frightening between where I am and where I want to be. Because of all I may become I will close my eyes and leap."

I brought the letter to a close and posted it. Soon a photocopy of that letter came back to me. The jump phrase was circled in red, with his note written in the margin: "THIS sentence, these words, are the reason you are ready to start your business now. You know everything you need to know . . . and these words should go on one of your first products."

They did.

I have heard stories over the years of how that particular sentence has been the motivation to move people along and give them the courage to put wings to their dreams.

Ha!

Just today I could fold those words into a letter, whispered after these words, "I am on the cusp of a remarkable journey. All the longings of my life have led me to this amazing transition in my experience."

Ah, yes. Jump.

Dream/Lead Like you know where you're going

It took some amount of negotiating to persuade the young intellectual from Germany to be my guest at that night's performance. We were both guests at the same London bed-and-breakfast, and he had made his very serious views toward life known each morning. While he insisted that musicals were frivolous and a waste of time, he concurred thriftily that not using my second ticket, which I had accidentally purchased, would be a waste of money.

That night both our views toward life shifted. We sat in a West End theater watching Hugo's story line unfold in *Les Misérables*. As the character of Fantine wept over her lost love and life in the song "I Dreamed a Dream," the heart in my guest seemed to be breaking. He was so visibly moved by the spectacle before him and increasingly understood that it was anything but frivolous. Watching this transformation in him, I resolved never to be so achingly in the grasp of a system of rigid assumptions. That musical became my soundtrack for many years. I cannot speak of the standing of that young man's life now, but I know that night he was the first to get to his feet as the curtain signaled the close. With hands above his head, he wept for the wonder. He saw that what he had thought was one thing (frivolous musicals) was something else entirely.

Was it a dream I held for that young man . . . or simply an accident that I purchased two tickets instead of one? Was I manifesting leadership for his life or just not paying attention? At the end of the matter, the result is answer enough for these questions.

As the audience stilled from their wild applause and moved to exit the theater, I was reminded of the wisdom of Mary Ann Evans (aka George Eliot) who courageously embraced her dream and passion saying, "It is never too late to become who you might have been." Said another way, "Continue to live toward your dream—the ultimate embrace of it will be worth your journey."

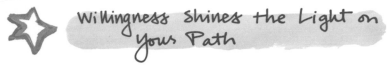

Willingness Shines the Light on your Path

The young executive spoke at length about her wish to trade her career for full-time mothering, to set aside her career away from home in order to stay home and make a career of raising her three-year-old. As she expressed these sentiments, she burst into tears. I recognized this as a sure way to be certain of our purpose—when just to speak them out loud is so filled with longing that it draws a sob from deep within the belly. Many people tend not to face their longings for this very reason—the discomfort of acknowledging such passion. Instead they walk along the river of their dreams on the opposite side, only occasionally stealing glances at what they deeply hope.

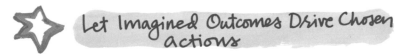

Let Imagined Outcomes Drive Chosen actions

He must have been nine. He was tall and slight of build. He was sporting a fleece cape, complete with fancy collar. "Wow," I exclaimed, as he strode past. "It's not every day you meet a superhero." Unsmiling, he nodded, acknowledging the truth of my statement. To confirm, I asked, "Are you really a superhero?" Stoically, he nodded that yes, he was. "Wow, may I have your autograph?" He stared at me. His face registered disbelief at the audacity of my question. With no further hesitation and holding my glance, he replied no. With that, he turned on his tennis-shoed-heel and walked away. He mother apologetically shrugged and trudged off behind him.

Hmmm. That is probably a good thing to know, I thought. Real superheroes don't give autographs.

 **Winged Thoughts**

Hold open your hands and raise them high. Dreams have a habit of raining on unexpected days . . . be prepared to catch as many as possible.

In the world of yes! possible and impossible are spelled the same way: d-r-e-a-m.

Here is what the crow teaches: flight is a certainty and soaring is inevitable.

What wonder there is in watching masterful designs chaotically recreate themselves into the beauty on the other side of imagination.

There are many ways to follow the truth of your dreams, but first you must be intimate with what your dreams are.

If you would dream it, start it; if you have an idea, open it; if there is longing, acknowledge it; if there is mission, commit it; if there is daring, risk it; if there is love, show it; if there is resource, use it; if there is abundance, share it.

Our days offer some pretty sizzling, demanding distractions to our true purpose, to keep us from our true dreams.

Winged Thoughts

So often what we think we should fear is not the real threat. The real threat is the cold embrace of fear around our heart of promise.

I begin to see my capacity for a thing as soon as I am open to believing my capacity, "I can do this."

Willingness, sometimes called risk, accompanies me in the finest service and is often led by a dream.

Believing opens your eyes to wisps of possibilities as they fold into whispers of promise, turn into statements of certainty, and end the day with shouts of glory and celebration.

You see your promise when you believe it can be, will be, is present; then the rest seems so simple and you wonder why you waited so long to believe.

Every possibility, each opportunity can stand at the threshold with the companion of "what if" . . . risk is the best response to that question.

Dreams, being real and simple and unfoldingly true, belong in our dance and the lightness of our being.

Have the presence to reinvent yourself and live the life you've been dreaming of.

Work because you can. Create because you must. Hold both elements tenderly in the precious dream.

Embrace the expanse of your dream and prepare a place for it in your day.

Let go of the small, "is," in favor of the larger, "if . . . "

Winged Thoughts

Be willing to be who you are in full measure: awake or dreaming.

These are your dreams. While they may wander unte-thered and all around the acreage of your experience, you must always call them home for supper. Call them your "dear ones, your sweet ones" . . . as you remember them back to their home and put them to rest. Promise them, no matter how far away they wander, you will always claim them as your own.

Walk into the opportunity of the day with an open hand and a willing heart—observe the alchemy as destiny meets up with disciplines and intuitions.

Possibility: a new roadway that is paved with dreams and willingness.

Love to learn, envision great action, and daily serve the dream.

Word Birds

Promises to Myself •••••

Dreaming requires courage. The courage to believe you know where you're going. When really it would be more accurate to say you know that you are going toward your dream . . . without the dream having precise or recognizable shape. The closer we get, the easier it is to recognize the dream. Explore the nature of your dream by making such a promise.

See Words

The greatest thing a human soul ever does in this world is to see something and tell what it saw in a plain way. Hundreds of people can talk for one who can think, but thousands can think for one who can see. To see clearly is poetry, prophecy, and religion all in one.
—John Ruskin

- I promise to look with clear sight at what I create.
- "Be a servant to your craft today."
- TODAY—no clocks, no timers, no editing. Every idea will be welcomed. All things considered . . .

Imagine Freely

It's not unrealistic planning—it's reality in training.
—mar

- I promise to let goodness soar in my soul.

- "Let's get this party started!"
- TODAY—look and see bigger; allow all possibilities to be considered; imagine fiercely and then double it.

Engage Possibility

The moment one gives close attention to anything,
even a blade of grass, it becomes a mysterious, awesome,
indescribably magnificent world in itself.
—Henry Miller

- I promise to stretch the realm of what appears possible.
- "Engage with the same wonder as a child."
- TODAY—everything is yes until it's no; observe a large sea of possibility, not an overwhelming collection of events; engage with all you can handle and walk past the rest.

Please Yourself

I don't know the key to success
but the key to failure is trying to please everybody.
—Bill Cosby

- I promise to validate my own creation.
- "Do what you must."
- TODAY—Say no to the non-essentials and say yes to what is essential; give full attention, without apology, and savor the joy of your purpose in action.

chapter 10

generosity

Live as if this is all there is

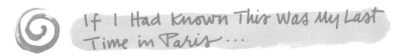 If I Had Known This Was My Last
Time in Paris . . .

My friend laughingly waved her dark chocolate at me saying, "Maybe if this was going to be the last time I'd ever see you, I'd share this with you." I didn't mean to wring all the funny out of the moment, but the words that immediately poured over my lips were "How do you know it isn't the last time you'll see me?" We were both stunned into silence from the impact of that single sentence. As outcomes go, this worked out pretty well for me. I got some chocolate, and I have seen her since.

Many years ago I was flippant in my visit to Paris. I anticipated that I would return again that fall. I did not. Nor have I in the many autumns that have since come and gone. So few of us have the capacity to sense with accuracy coming events. So each day, what might change if we considered that this might be all there is . . .

I've experienced this in practice while supporting my friend through her battle with several types of cancer at various stages of progression. I've observed how much more easily "I love you" occurs in her conversations. Pointed remarks and truthful observation are delivered with tenderness and absent any apology. I've watched her learn to disavow caring much for the opinions of others in regard to her choices at all levels. The reality of her health has imposed the realization that each day might, indeed, be her last. It's been excellent exercise for the fullness of life stretching before her.

At last tally, it was Cancer 5 and D. R. 17. On her road to wellness, she's not resorting to taking things for granted. Oh, no. If anything, she is more committed than ever to being fully present to the needs that appear in the day. And it's been part of her lesson to realize that the most important needs to address begin and end with caring for her own health. Such a view has taken practice. And she has taken on the practice much like an athlete preparing for competition.

The Muscle That Builds With Use

It's a funny thing about life;
if you refuse to accept anything but the best you very often get it.
—W. Somerset Maugham

Jan Johnson, author and Red Wheel/Weiser and Conari Press publisher, has a profound capacity to condense truth. She summarizes my thoughts in this way, "Expect the best. Give your best and get the best." In this view, instead of just muscle building, the process is also circular. Maybe the circle expands as you practice. And Jan's view supports the familiar phrase, "What goes around comes around."

A particular day comes to mind in which I faced disappointment at several corners. Important calls missed, mail absent a promised payment, news of another economic failure here in our own democracy. These disappointments cast an interesting light on my understanding of Maugham's words and Jan's assertion.

Repeatedly, I have seen what I thought was "the best thing" turn out to be the worst possible choice. I have also determined, in advance of an event, my sense of how it would go in the best scenario and have been utterly taken in delight by something completely different than I anticipated. As my husband and I strategized and anticipated our next home, I found myself setting aside specifics, an unusual step for me, and advocating that I hope for a few specifics and will let the rest unfold. With the push-push-push of a specific and rigid agenda, the "best" can accidentally be rejected when it shows up . . . because it did not look like or meet the identified set of expectations.

So we held a loosely framed set of hopes and moved into a home that far exceeded what either of us imagined.

I am reminded in so many ways that to live as if this is all there is allows the circumstances of the day to present themselves as the best the day has to offer. In turn, I aspire to offer my best to the day. And that seems to draw a beneficial circle.

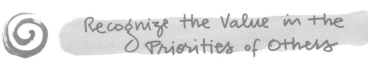

Recognize the Value in the Priorities of Others

I can stop to see you. I am able to pause what I am doing to see what is important to you. Recently, while visiting the California Academy of Sciences, I saw a mom taking a photo of her two daughters. "Would you like to be in the picture?" "Oh, yes!" she said as she handed me her camera without hesitation. Two lovely daughters, an enthused mom, and two disinterested stuffed zebras later, I handed her digital camera back. She looked with approval at the image that registers immediately. "Oh, that's good. Thank you." I returned to my cadence and a friend who said, "That's a mitzvah." Mitzvah brought to mind the lyrical recitation "No sadness, no sadness. It is a mitzvah to forget the gloom."

A mitzvah. A good deed performed out of a sense of religious, or spiritual duty. The definition differs and expands for me: a mitzvah is a positive act intended as an investment in goodness and joy—both my own and others.

A Single Generosity Enlarges the World

One bold inspiration choreographs a dance with promise. One unlike-lihood entertained leads a parade of innovation. One whispered *yes* becomes the wind song over an ocean of no's. One service to need heals an ancient wound. One movement toward light becomes a clear signpost on a long road. A small compassionate act enlarges the scope of community.

Teachers or any professionals might be tempted to ask if their purpose on the planet might be a level deeper than originally thought. An initial thought is we are here to inspire many others. What if it's really to inspire the few who will, in turn, inspire the many? Or, more to the point, to influence one who will, in turn, change the world. Today may be that day. Your one day to have that single most important influence on the life of another human being.

Judgment and weariness are foes to service and generosity.

In service, there is clarity and compassion to override those two forces of negativity. Judgment is discernment on a bad hair day. Weariness comes, on some days, from lack of service to self. When I was finished pouring my heart into a presentation, I was supposed to be signing books. More to the point, the host of the event expected me to be selling books. So many people wanted to engage questions and tell their stories. I had to make a choice. I listened to the stories. Would these same people have been compelled to tell these very same stories to any speaker who had addressed them? I will never know. I only know that they chose to tell me and I stood still. I set down my commercial obligations, and I served the souls who had stories to tell. I listened as she wove her story.

A lost child. A broken dream. A dream realized. Art discovered. And on August 21, 1968, Russian tanks roared into Prague, changing one life forever. In 1973 she immigrated to her freedom in America. On Thanksgiving Day. I still hear her words ringing in my ears, "The first thanksgiving served all who were immigrants. Many Americans do not know or have forgotten what it is to come here new. That was a real Thanksgiving in 1973, and it is, every year since."

I could have judged the talking ones to be at odds with my requirements. My weariness could have cut short my capacity to entertain the "next" story. Those foes set down, I listened. And every Thanksgiving since is a richer experience for that service.

Just How Busy Are You?

Greetings to You,

You always hear from me, but I thought I'd officially notify you today on behalf of expectation, uncertainty, self-recrimination, and resistance. We are involved in a significant meeting. Since everybody knows me as the Busy Mind, they figured asking me to do "one more thing" wouldn't matter.

"Bring it on! I can do it all—even though I already have so much to do." Yes. That's really me talking when those martyr-like phrases come out of your mouth. Well, anyway, I'm speaking on their behalf today.

You, left to your own devices, just play with delight and create from your heart. Thank God! I'm there to remind you of all your responsibilities, strengths, and shortcomings. See, I try for balance in my whispering. No wonder you've been tucking your head into those little electronic word games. You can't hear me there. It really bugs me when you do that, by the way. When you come out of the soundproof booth, I have to up my game just to bring you up to speed.

Look, it's our collective jobs to keep you connected to everything. All that "letting go" stuff you practice just keeps us all damn busy running around, catching the stuff, and bringing it back to you. If you'd just hold on to stuff in the first place, it would make all of our jobs so much easier. (You're just lucky I haven't endorsed a union here. You would really have a hard time shutting us out then.) Just keep in mind that we are committed—we will do whatever it takes to keep you mired in our realities.

I wish you'd give up this focus phrase process of yours. That's another thing that makes our jobs super-hard. How's a busy mind supposed to be effective when your mind is open, at ease, and simply observing and learning from the world around you? I'm the Conduit. I want to be in charge, and I want you to let me be in charge.

Yeah, yeah, everybody—I know! Everybody here wants to think that they are in charge. Fine. You all can think what you want.

Okay, okay, I'll communicate for them now.

Fear says he's only trying to protect you from making the same mistakes. "Hey, wait a minute! Fear, when did you show up to this meeting? I hate it when you slip in late without me noticing."

Expectation says she's only trying to help you live up to your astonishingly well-polished standard-trophies. Uncertainty reminds you he's actually creativity in disguise—but he doesn't want you to get all soft and cushy in your career so he dresses up as uncertainty. (You know this already, right? Seriously? How do you forget a thing like that? Maybe I've fallen down on my job by not helping you remember this.)

Self-recrimination. Before I let you hear from that department, let me just say that self-recrimination has been a real management challenge for me. She often steps in trying to do my job. Imagine. Her! Trying to sound like the Busy Mind. But she's actually been pulling it off quite a bit lately. So help me watch out for that, okay?

All right. Self-recrimination, my underling, my employee, self-recrimination who reports first to me, not to you—just wants you to know she knew you before everybody else. She knew you when you were just an obscure nobody. Who would keep you humble if she didn't?

Resistance is the head of the Internal Corps of Engineers. He's very busy right now so he left right after we started this meeting. But I can tell you what's what. He understands your lack of artistic discipline. He sees how you've succumbed to the process of designing by fire—large bonfire bursts. So he just steps in and digs those fire line trenches as deep as he can. By the time the fire is large enough to breach the line, it is roaring and unstoppable.

I know. I know. It leaves you exhausted. But that's one of my busiest times. I get to keep you engaged with all the other things you haven't done while creative fire building.

See? We really do all work hard for you. So if you could stop this being present, in joy, with the present moment nonsense, it would go a lot better for all of us.

There is so much more I could say—but I've got a lot to do so I've got to go. Take care.

With earnest regard,
    —The Busy Mind

Seen or unseen, there is, indeed, a world of grace that exists alongside my own. I give little study and much gratitude to the world of otherness. I recognize the angels on the road in my experiences. I neither define nor defend them.

On my most contented, centered days, I sense an almost playful exchange with the company of beings. And on other days, I am embarrassed at my acknowledgment of this presence of unseen others. It is not academic. It is not particularly demonstrable, but by anecdotal tale. I can't open a cupboard to present my collection of angels nor can I prescribe a meeting place or schedule their appearance in my planning book. No, I find them only when I am open in my heart to the holy opportunity of a single precious moment.

> A smile changes each encounter to a greater likelihood of joy or possibility.

We shall never know all the good that a simple smile can do.
—Mother Teresa

The first good we can know is the good that it does for us. Those of us who are offering the smile.

Smiling changes perspective. A smile changes each encounter to a greater likelihood of joy or possibility or at least something pleasant.

My smile can come readily, but today it wasn't simply an unconscious response. I smiled at everyone today because I was reflecting on Mother Teresa's phrase. It turned out to be the equivalent to an all-day pass at everyone's gates. I spoke at length with several strangers. And even a few dogs, too.

I have no way of knowing, with any certainty, the good that my all-day smiles did for others. I know, without a doubt, what good it did for me.

 Winged Thoughts

Didtionary. My life: defined by my actions. My life: defined by my dreams. My *Didtionary.*

Even if it is my last road, I am willing to walk an utterly new road.

The press of time makes surprised fools out of all of us.

Encased between the quote marks of our weeks are the dreams we repeat in our sleep but hesitate to realize when we are awake.

Actively living with the question "Does *this* really matter?" changes every little thing.

Give and receive equally well.

Hands open, facing upward, acting on the impulse to give; saying thank-you easily when gifted, recognizing that gifts are often intangibles.

I will not measure my abundance by what I have in the bank, but, rather, by what I am able to share with those who are in immediate need.

Define yourself by your living, not by the possibility (inevitability) of dying.

Winged Thoughts

The greatest investment in a day is a dangerous unselfishness wrapped in joy and tied with ribbons of laughter and learning, understanding and compassion. (Thanks to Dr. Martin Luther King Jr. for the inspiration of the phrase "dangerous unselfishness.")

Seize your days with a fierce tenacity and relish.

When I choose to hold tightly to what I perceive are my venues of opportunity, there is no open door, no way for entry of surprise. When I hold possibility in an open hand, I am both poised to give and prepared to receive.

Life is a song, and the most beautiful lyrics are the generosities in my days.

It is your own story you tell by the actions of your day.

It is not "What next?" but "What *now*?"

Every moment is the opportunity for a fresh start, a new day.

The best work is paired with a desire to serve, and our finest effort partners with dreams for joy and bringing comfort over the long road.

This moment is the explicit poetry of my life.

Enjoy your blink.

Abundance is simply being generous with your good fortune.

Joy gets lost in the machinations of "doing" and evaluating what "could have gone better." Savor praise given for any moment.

Trust and willingness are the foundation of a meaningful life.

Making memories . . . ask yourself, "How is it I would like to remember this day?"

Have a long memory for joys and a short memory for disappointments.

Please yourself

Promises to Myself • • • • •

Do you wonder how your day might be different if you lived it as if this is all there is? Explore your own answer by making a promise that asks the question.

Let Loose

Eat the present moment and break the dish.
—Egyptian proverb

• I promise to let go and soar.

• "Transform. Create, cry, or sing because the beauty compels you. Scream, shout, or take action because hands still hurt children and people think dogs do not understand a cage. Live like there's no tomorrow."

• TODAY—reflect on the year; be ordinary, be extraordinary, and know there's just a little difference; do what you know and be willing to learn what you do not know.

Right Timing

Time is the coin of your life. It is the only coin you have,
and only you can determine how it will be spent.
Be careful lest you let other people spend it for you.
—Carl Sandburg

• I promise to patiently embrace the natural progression of things.

• "Things really do unfold or transform in their own time."

• TODAY—follow the pattern of the season in your day; flow not push; call them targeted completion dates, not deadlines; take a walk and think of Carl Sandburg . . .

Reciprocal graces

There is no small kindness;
every compassionate act makes large the world.

—mar

• I promise to give and receive equally well.

• "Accept with the same grace that you give."

• Looking into this day, this might mean—hands open, facing upward, acting readily on the impulse to give; saying thank-you easily when gifted with anything; recognizing that gifts are often intangibles.

Deep Beliefs (one Thing)

I get up every morning determined to both change the world
and have one hell of a good time.

—E. B. White

• I promise to connect to my deepest beliefs and act on my *one thing*.

• "In spite of circumstances, be buoyed by your *one thing*."

• Looking into my day, this might mean—being connected to my beliefs/meaning in all my actions; preparing and packaging holiday gifts with love; allowing my intentions their practical application in the day and being encouraged, in the large, by my intentions, not discouraged in the small, by disappointments.

No Hurry

Stepping aside from habit makes room for the fresh winds of power.
—mar

• I promise to not rush through the many requirements of my day.

• "Pace yourself, enjoy the 'list,' and allow 'good enough' to seem like perfection."

• Looking into this day, this might mean—not getting revved up; walking on purpose rather than driving; passing on nonessential actions; ha! not taking a shower.

I thought the drama was when the actors cried,
but the drama is when the audience cries.
—Frank Capra

The butterfly counts not months but moments, and has time enough.
—Rabindranath Tagore

You never have to change anything
you got up in the middle of the night to write.
—Saul Bellow

afterword

The gas tank started beeping the empty sound, and the car almost didn't start. It took three tries, but gas finally got to the engine. I smiled first and then laughed. That engine and that fuel line are something like the days I am experiencing. Pretty close to running on empty but enough to get me to the pump.

Then I just smiled thinking about the long road my life has taken on the way to "the pump."

I pulled out of the driveway considering the complexity and paradoxes of my life as an author and artist. What a contradiction it is to have people turning to me, asking, "How?" Like I really know the answers to so many different questions that all begin with "How?" "How do you walk through the tough times while keeping an inspired view?" "How do you manage to keep a writing discipline on a daily basis?" How. H O W. Until it all begins to sound like howls.

And my primal response to the howling is "You gotta look at the rest of the pack and then find your own howl. You can listen to all the other sounds, but, ultimately, the sound that rises up from the bottom of your belly and rides up through your upraised throat and spills over your lips is your sound. Your howl. I can only tell you how I make my noise. It can inspire you to make your own noise. But be assured it must be your own."

I stopped at the light across from the gas station. "The pump." I thought about Brother Lawrence, that fifteenth-century monk who respected liturgy but didn't have much use for it. He called washing dishes his prayer. Serving breakfast to his brother in the best way possible was his prayer. Facing grunt work with grace—prayer. This is want I want to underscore in my writing. Not that I have the answer, but that I so long to inspire my reader to find and celebrate their answers. "That's the real key, isn't it?" I asked myself as I pulled into the gas station.

And there I am. A little dog in the car enthusiastically supporting my actions as I leave the car. She watches my every move. I see the love in her eyes. But she's not doing it for me. In physical ways, she's not even helping me. She's cheerleading but not even paying for part of the gas! I wonder if this is what my relationship to Spirit is like. I wonder if that's why dogs are such resonant relationships for me.

> I long for this book to be an experience that meets readers at many different levels.

They are a model for how my life plays out with Spirit. (I laugh again, musing that people often point out that *dog* is *God* spelled backward.)

I fill the tank. Gas is more expensive on the island, and I might be near a Costco on Sunday. It's less expensive there. Maybe I should just put a quarter of a tank in. I contemplate the thoughts of the hard start less than a mile back. I decide to fill my tank and let it lead the metaphor in the day. Demonstrate that, at least, while I certainly cannot meet all the obligations in the day, I have enough in the moment. My basics are utterly fulfilled and on some days that is the biggest celebration.

I drive to my studio thinking about the final effort I am pouring into this work, that I want this book to be an *event*. I want the Word Birds to be a resource of inspiration. The Promises to Myself to provide a model for readers to begin making their own promises and fulfilling them on a daily basis. I long for this book to be an experience that meets readers at many different levels. To point to their own discoveries, their own finest intentions, and serve as a beautiful reminder that there are so many ways to walk to goodness . . . but the finest way is the way that readers choose and craft for themselves.

Waiting for me at my studio is an email message from my earth-connected friend, Barb. The woman who, even in her greatest challenges, can still hear the promise in the soil and still knows that miracles wait in every seed, in every womb, in every wisp that is blown on a chilled spring breeze. Her friend Victory sent these words to her, and she, in turn, like the seed on the wind, cast them in the cyber breeze to me. I share them with you, my precious readers, because this poem, better than any of my own, expresses the very idea I was wondering how to communicate.

Prayers Like Shoes

I wear prayers like shoes

pull em on quiet each morning
take me through the uncertain day

don't know
what might knock me off course

sit up in bed
pull on the right
then the left
before shower before teeth

my mama's gift
to walk me through this life
she wore strong ones
the kind steady your ankles
i know
cause when her man left/ her children

gone/ her eldest son without goodbye
they the only ones keep her
standing

i saw her
still standing

mama passed on
some things to me
ma smile sense a discipline
ma
subtle behind

but best she passed on
girl you go to God
and get you some good shoes
cause this life ain't steady ground

now i don't wear hers
you take em with you you know
but i suspect they made by the same company
pull em on each morning
first the right   then the left

best piece a dress
i got

Ruth Forman, from *Prayers Like Shoes*

In even what appear to be the most difficult experiences of our lives, there are synergistic events that offer us support and comfort. I used to explain that crossroads of things as an intersection where silence and words meet. I'd suggest that intersection is where poetry is born. Our days are made up of such intersecting patterns, lines, lyrics, lessons, intentions, apparent coincidences. This book, a narrative of my life, the stories I repeat, is simply my effort to make sense of that which might decline to be explained.

And so it is that we must agree that much of our lives is mystery. And we get to meet that mystery wrapped in our intentions and engaged with our brightest hopes and deepest willingness. When we come to the dawn of our awakening day, holding our own well-cultivated and (re)discovered intentions, we move with an unparalleled grace. And in movement or stillness, discovery or our uncertain mystery, we still hold the flame of our one thing high, that we may, at the very least, light the path in front of our own feet, with our own good shoes, and, at best, shed a little light for some other walker.

embrace your strengths

acknowledgments

David Lee Gordon, Barb (*www.bellaterrasilver.com*), D. R., Molly shannon (*www.mollyshannonneel.com*), Dr. Deanna Davis (*www .deannadavis.net*), Kim Hamilton (*mudlark.com*) and Barbara Joy (*parentingwithjoy.com*)—thank you for letting me take our personal stories and exchanges and share them with an audience.

Steve Maraboli (*www.stevemaraboli.com*)—your vision and enthusiasm are a gift in my life. Thank you for generously letting me share your words with my readers.

Ruth Forman (*ruthforman.com*), whose words brought unexpected tears of recognition and whose grace humbles me. Thank you for the generosity of your words in this book. Sandra Grace (*sandragrace .com*)—thank you for your ten things.

Conari Press, you make a fine dance partner and I am grateful for the ways you bring my words to the world; Liz, for the beauty and ease you bring when you put your artful hand to my art; Jan, especially for the generosity with your time when it is a premium commodity.

And to my readers who say to their friends, "You've got to read this book . . ." time and again, I thank you for allowing me the privilege of earning my livelihood with work that I am so passionate about. I would not be able to do this without you.

To Our Readers

Conari Press, an imprint of Red Wheel/Weiser, publishes books on topics ranging from spirituality, personal growth, and relationships to women's issues, parenting, and social issues. Our mission is to publish quality books that will make a difference in people's lives--how we feel about ourselves and how we relate to one another. We value integrity, compassion, and receptivity, both in the books we publish and in the way we do business.

Our readers are our most important resources, and we value your input, suggestions, and ideas about what you would like to see published. Please feel free to contact us, to request our latest book catalog, or to be added to our mailing list.

Conari Press
An imprint of Red Wheel/Weiser, LLC
500 Third Street, Suite 230
San Francisco, CA 94107
www.redwheelweiser.com